METHODICAL
BIBLE
STUDY

METHODICAL
BIBLE
STUDY

Robert A. Traina

ZONDERVAN™

GRAND RAPIDS, MICHIGAN 49530

ZONDERVAN™

Methodical Bible Study
Copyright © 1952, 1980 by Robert A. Traina

First Francis Asbury Press printing 1985.

Requests for information should be addressed to:
Zondervan, *Grand Rapids, Michigan 49530*

ISBN 0-310-24602-4

Printed in the United States of America

HB 11.22.2023

FOREWORD

"How DUSTY IS your Bible?" might be asked of many a person who would be ashamed not to own a Bible but to whom it is an unknown book, beyond a few characters, some chapters, and scattered verses heard from others.

Professor Robert A. Traina in the book he has written has inspired the reader to remove the dust, open the Scriptures, and come to know the joyous adventure to be found in studying the great variety of literature in the Old and New Testaments by following some definite plan of study. The intellectual stimulus, the spiritual inspiration, and the urge to share the experience with others to be gained from following the instructions of this book will repay hours of effort. The author does not suggest the easy way such as "passing the apple sauce," but the more stimulating one of "planting trees" and discovering for oneself the great and hidden treasures of the literature of the centuries as found in the Bible.

The author is qualified as a scholar to lead the way in method, since he excelled as a student himself at The Biblical Seminary in New York. He has also been a teacher who has inspired his students to teach others. Included in these are men and women who today are in demand in other countries as well as in the United States among university and other students who wish to be led into a stimulating and satisfying approach to the Bible.

The reader should keep constantly in mind the principle which is basic to the purpose of this book, namely, that the study of method is not an end in itself but a means to an

end. In fact, it should be remembered that the Scriptures
themselves are only a "signpost to the house of shelter" leading to a closer relationship with the living Christ, who is the
Alpha and Omega, the Beginning and the End.

Professor William Lyon Phelps once said to his audience,
holding up the morning edition of the *New York Times*,
"The Bible is more up to date than this paper." Following
the suggestions of this book, one can easily prove such a
statement.

CAROLINE L. PALMER

New York, New York

May, 1952

AUTHOR'S NOTE

THE AUTHOR IS deeply indebted to many for the ideas contained herein. One of the chief of these is Dr. Caroline L. Palmer, who as his teacher is responsible for much of what he knows and who so kindly consented to write the foreword to this book.

It would be ideal if individual credit could be given at every point where it is due, but for obvious reasons this cannot be accomplished. However, it is the author's hope that this study will make a contribution toward achieving the objectives of those whose ideas he utilizes and thereby justify his liberal use of their discoveries.

CONTENTS

CONTENTS

INTRODUCTION

Page

INTRODUCTION

A. Why Did He Do It?—The Need and a Remedy

THERE ARE SOME intriguing similarities between a good detective and an efficient Bible student.

A good detective must be skilled in certain techniques, such as knowing where to look for clues and how to go about finding them. For example, he must be aware of the importance of such factors as finger printing and ballastic tests in relation to crime detection. And having found evidence, he must be able to interpret it properly, to piece it together to discover the pattern into which it falls, to evaluate it, and to draw valid conclusions from it. And in all this the good detective is systematic. He follows insofar as he is able an orderly process which he feels will best enable him to discover the criminal. By all means he avoids haphazardness, because he knows that haphazardness is not conducive to efficient detection.

The effective Bible student follows much the same course, because in many ways he is a Scriptural detective. He too must be adept at knowing what to look for and how to discover those facts which are necessary for understanding particular passages. He also must be able to ascertain the relations between the clues, to interpret them and to assess their worth accurately, and to make legitimate deductions. And in carrying out these steps it is just as important that the Bible student be methodical as it is for a detective.

And yet the fact is that too many students of the Scriptures approach their task as no good detective would, in a hit-and-miss, trial-and-error fashion. They have no orderly, well-thought-out plan of action. They tend to follow the whims of the moment.

This weakness exists not only among laymen, where it might be expected, but also among many who have had special training in the field of Bible study. One of the main reasons for this fact is that the need for methodicalness is not usually recognized, and consequently the student is not taught to analyze the process of interpretation in order to develop a thorough, logical, step-by-step approach which he may utilize in the exposition of any Scriptural passage. Some of the consequences of such a lack are wasted time, inaccuracy, and superficiality.

These and related convictions have led to the preparation of the forthcoming discussion, in which the writer presents a detailed analysis of the process of Bible study which has formed the basis for his personal attempt to develop a methodical approach to Scriptural passages. He has no illusions that this book contains a panacea which guarantees the cure of all the ills of Bible study. Nor does he expect that what he has found beneficial in his own thinking and work will be adopted *in toto* by the reader; for methodicalness, in the last instance, is an individual matter. However, it is hoped that in some small way this material will convey to the reader the concept of methodical Bible study, together with a sense of its importance. If this is accomplished, the time given to its preparation will have been well spent.

B.   What Is It?—Definition of Methodical Bible Study

Although the preceding statements have indicated something of the meaning of methodical Bible study, let us define it more thoroughly to insure clarity.

In discovering the meaning of the term "methodical," it will help us to examine first the definition of the noun "method." "Method" is based on the Greek word *methodos,* which literally means "a way or path of transit." In the light of its derivation, note carefully the following definitions of "method."

> Method may denote either an abstraction or a concrete procedure, but in both cases it implies orderly, logical, and effective arrangement, as of one's ideas for an exposition or an argument, or of the steps to be followed in teaching, in investigation . . . or in any kind or piece of work.[1]

> Method at bottom is but the way of doing things followed in any given case . . . The main steps that have to be taken . . . and the crucial points where conditions of growth have to be carefully maintained and fostered.[2]

Methodical Bible study, then, is concerned with the proper path to be taken in order to arrive at Scriptural truth. More specifically, it involves the discovery of those steps necessary for achieving its goal and their arrangement in a logical and effective manner.

To illustrate, one may draw an analogy between methodical Bible study and a cooking recipe. The following is a recipe for baking a gold cake. Note the parallels between it and methodical Bible study in view of the preceding definitions.

1. Grease and flour an 8 x 8 square pan
2. Sift together into mixing bowl
   1⅝ cups sifted flour
   1 cup sugar
   2 tsp. baking powder
   ½ tsp. salt
3. Add
   ⅓ cup shortening
4. Pour in
   ⅔ cup milk
   1 tsp. vanilla
5. Beat for 2 minutes
6. Add
   1 large egg
7. Beat for 2 additional minutes
8. Pour into prepared pan and bake for 30 minutes at 350°.

You undoubtedly observed how the recipe instructs one to follow certain steps, such as using particular ingredients, mixing them, and placing the batter in the oven at a certain temperature and for a certain length of time. These steps are essential if one is to bake this particular kind of cake. However, not only are these specific steps necessary, but it is also important that they be done in the order suggested. For if there were a *drastic* revision of the sequence so that the cake were baked before the batter was mixed, the outcome would be tragic. Likewise, methodical Bible study entails two indispensable factors: first, certain steps (content), and second, a certain arrangement (order). Neither of these can be sacrificed if one's approach is to be methodical. Therefore, the question to which we must address ourselves is a twofold one: "What steps must we follow and in what order of arrangement that we may realize our goal of effective Bible study?" [3]

C. What Is Behind It?—Basic Premises

There are certain postulates which underlie methodical Bible study. No attempt will be made to prove these conclusively, for even if this could be done it would necessitate one or more volumes in itself. The main purpose here is to state them as clearly and succinctly as possible.[4]

1. **The Bible Is Worth Studying.**

2. **Certain Factors Are Involved in the Methodical Study of the Scriptures.**

These will be discussed in terms of the characteristics of methodical Bible study.

a. *Inductive Bible Study*

One necessary requisite of a methodical approach is that it correspond in nature with its objective, for it is the means by which the objective is reached. Thus, for instance, the methodical approach to throwing a baseball would include, among other things, gripping the ball firmly, cocking the arm back, and propelling the ball by a forward flip of the arm. This is necessarily true because of the very nature of throwing a baseball. If, then, a particular approach to the Scriptures is to be valid, it must bear a substantial likeness to the Scriptures themselves.

Now the Scriptures are distinct from the interpreter and are not an integral part of him. If the truths of the Bible already resided in man, there would be no need for the Bible and this manual would be superfluous. But the fact is that *the Bible is an objective body of literature* which exists because man needs to know certain truths which he himself cannot know and which must come to him from without. Consequently, if he is to discover the truths which reside in this objective body of literature, he must utilize an approach which corresponds in nature with it, that is, an *objective* approach.

There are two main approaches open to the Bible student. One is deduction, which begins with generalizations and moves for their support to the particulars. By its very nature deduction tends to be subjective and prejudicial. It produces those who dictate to the Scriptures rather than those who listen to the Scriptures. In view of the objective character of Scriptural literature, such an approach is not suited to the Bible and is therefore unmethodical. On the other hand, its opposite, induction, is objective and impartial; for it demands that one first examine the particulars of the Scriptures and that one's conclusions be based on those particulars. Such an approach is sound because, being objective, it corresponds to the objective nature of the Scriptures. It produces hearers rather than speakers, and the nature of the Scriptures requires hearers. Methodical Bible study, then, is inductive Bible study, because in this instance induction is methodical.

Two qualifications should be made of this equation of methodicalness and induction. The first is that there is no such thing as pure induction. When one talks about an inductive approach, one means an approach which is relatively inductive. The same principle applies to deduction. The second is a consequence of the first. Because there is no pure induction, there is no absolute objectivity. Gamaliel Bradford wisely observed, "There are simply those who think they are impartial and those who know they are not." However, an approach which stresses induction insofar as is possible is more likely to produce impartial and accurate interpreters than any other approach.

b. *Direct, Independent Bible Study*

Granted that induction represents the methodical approach to the Scriptures, the question arises as to the exact means of discovering the particular facts upon which one's conclusions must be grounded.

It seems reasonable to assume that the best way to insure finding the particulars is to make a direct and independent study of the particulars themselves. Thus the Bible itself and not books about the Bible should be the basic textbook of the Bible student. Such an emphasis on the primacy of firsthand observation enables the interpreter to become acquainted with the spirit of Scriptural authors,[5] makes possible original thinking, and provides him with a basis for judging the validity of various and often conflicting secondary sources.

This stress on the primacy of firsthand study does not imply that an examination of commentaries is not recommended. On the contrary, when done in the proper place, it is recognized as an indispensable step in a methodical approach. Spurgeon rightly indicates that "two opposite errors beset the student of the Scriptures: the tendency to take everything second hand from others, and the refusal to take anything from others." [6]

Since there are many forms of the Bible, there is a need to decide which should be used. The choice is determined by the requirements of the individual interpreter; for if he himself must search out the particulars, he must be given a tool which he is capable of using. Thus in most instances the Bible in the mother tongue is best suited for the initial phase of inductive study. This is true because the average Bible student is not expert enough in the original languages to handle them with any great amount of authority. And since the translations are the work of experts in the field, it is quite certain that most students of the Scriptures will not be able to improve on them, at least not very much. Furthermore, a person thinks in his mother tongue and is therefore able to learn best when he is handling the vernacular. There is also the fact that the mother tongue enables one to see broad relations in a way virtually impossible when using the original languages. For these and other reasons the forthcoming discussion will be based on the conviction that the first step in a methodical approach to the Scriptures should be a direct and independent study of the vernacular. This in no way implies a failure to recognize the invaluable assistance provided by the use of the original. On the other hand, one finds that the direct and independent use of the vernacular often enhances one's interest in and knowledge of the original. [7]

c. Literary Bible Study

Literary Bible study assumes that the Scriptures consist of outstanding literature and that they are therefore governed by the laws which control all great literature. These facts make it imperative that the student of the Scriptures be conversant with and guided by the laws of literature. V. Ferm states:

The Bible as a whole is great literature, and a study
of the greatness in books, of the nature of poetic
genius and its creations, is at least as necessary for
the real understanding of the book as is the training of the historical critic.[8]

It should be noted that this premise is based on the conviction that though the Scriptures are unique in content and
message, they are similar to other literature in form, since
they too involve written linguistic communication. If this is
true, then literary form performs the same functions in relation to Biblical ideas as it does in relation to non-Biblical
ideas, that is, it is the means of communication and consequently the means of interpretation. It is therefore necessary
that one take into account the literary qualities of the Scriptures if one's approach is to be methodical.

d. *Psychological Bible Study*

The Bible is no abstract text on religion, nor is it an
almanac of religious facts and beliefs. It is a record of living,
dynamic religious experience. It is psychological in nature.
Therefore, the interpreter's approach must always take into
account the experiential aspect of the Scriptures. V. Ferm
precedes the statement quoted above with these words:

Much of the Bible, Old Testament and New, has
the character of poetry, and much that is not fully
poetic in form is yet inspired by deep emotion and
has the quality of greatness as literature. I found
it rewarding to approach the Bible with the assumption that it is great literature, that it is to be
enjoyed and not only understood, or rather that it
cannot be really understood unless one adds to a
knowledge of outward facts, which may help us to
see each book in its original place and immediate
purpose, a sympathetic insight into the mind and
soul of its author, an understanding which should

be less a knowledge of things than a knowledge of persons by a person.[9]

e. Constructive Bible Study

Someone has well noted, "These are times in which whatsoever is of boundless dimensions in Holy Scriptures has passed beyond our range of vision while our spectacled eyes are on iotas." Because of the presence of this tendency and the dangers inherent in it, it is imperative that we as Bible students concentrate on what is positive and clear and obviously fundamental. Problems there are in the interpretation of the Scriptures, but they need not and must not occupy the major share of our time. For as someone has observed, it is not the parts of the Bible we do not understand that ought to bother us, but the parts we do understand.

f. Comprehensive Bible Study

Ideally, methodical Bible study should be thorough in two respects: first, in *means*—every helpful means should be used in the study of Scriptural truth; and second, in *scope*—there should be a complete mastery of the Scriptures in view of the purpose of each book and of the entire Bible.[10]

g. Sincere Bible Study

This characteristic was involved in the discussion of induction, but it is so important it can bear repetition. In approaching the Scriptures one ought "to put nothing into them, but rather draw everything from them and suffer nothing to remain hidden which is really in them." [11] In his *Introduction to Shakespeare*, Hardin Craig remarks:

> There seemed only one honest way to proceed. I have had to clear the field where it needed clearing, and I have done so in the faith that, if we can by those means hear Shakespeare's voice, there is nothing further to worry about.

As Bible students we likewise must approach the Scriptures with the purpose of allowing them to speak, and with the faith that if we can but hear their voice, there is nothing further to worry about. L. Gilman said of Toscanini:

> Toscanini unconsciously reminds us that only those artists can touch the deepest springs who manifest their single-mindedness, their purity of intention, their incorruptible sincerity.[12]

Only those manifesting these same qualities will realize their true functions as students of the Word.

h. Assimilative Bible Study

The immediate purpose of Bible study in relation to the participants is that they reproduce the experience which in the first place produced the Scriptures. The Chinese student who wrote, "I am now reading the Bible and behaving it," caught the import of this basic principle. It is essential that the truth discovered in the Bible be thus incorporated into life. This is true for many reasons, two of which we shall note.

First, the assimilation of Scriptural truth is that which makes Bible study worthwhile. Holbrook Jackson, in his book entitled *The Reading of Books*, says:

> The primary effect of reading is awakening, not informing . . . Unless in some way or at some time words, sentences, or books explode thus beneficently and creatively, not only revealing life but showing us how to live, reading is a waste of time.

Such a statement is especially true in relation to the study of the Bible.

Second, the appropriation of Scriptural truth leads to increasing insight, whereas the failure to do so results in spiritual atrophy. Jesus made this abundantly clear in connection with the parables He spoke:

> If any man has ears to hear, let him hear. Take heed what you hear; the measure you give will be the measure you get, and still more will be given you. For to him who has will more be given; and from him who has not, even that which he has will be taken away. (Mark 4:23-25.)

i. *Reverent Bible Study*

Reverence is necessary for two main reasons.

First, it makes possible receptivity, and receptivity is essential for understanding spiritual truth. Jesus Himself taught this fact in the parable of the soils. (Mark 4:1-20.) Horace Bushnell once observed:

> My experience is that the Bible is dull when I am dull. When I am really alive and set upon the text with a tidal pressure of living affinities, it opens, it multiplies discoveries, and reveals depths even faster than I can note them.

Dullness in Bible study is due to an improper attitude toward the Scriptures and can be overcome only by the development of a true respect for them.

Second, it involves a prayerful dependence upon the Spirit of God, without Whom one cannot understand the Word; for He who inspired the Word is also its supreme interpreter. Bushnell adds to the statement quoted above, "The worldly spirit shuts out the Bible; the Spirit of God makes it a fire flaming out all-meaning and glorious truths." [13]

D.   How Shall I Use It?—A List of Suggestions

Since prevention is usually better than a cure, an attempt will be made at this juncture to anticipate some of the problems which usually arise, in order better to prepare the reader for understanding and using the forthcoming material. This will be done in terms of a list of miscellaneous suggestions.

1. Try to see the methodical process of study as-a-whole before attempting to apply any of its parts. Such perspective is necessary because of the interrelatedness of the various steps. They are so interdependent that it is impossible to understand the function of any one of them without knowing its relation to what precedes and follows. Consequently, the reader is urged to study the entire manual before trying to utilize its suggestions or even before making a serious attempt to understand fully any of its parts. Furthermore, advantage should be taken of the outlines which precede the various sections in order to note carefully their contents and organization. In these ways the reader will be enabled to see the interrelations between the steps and thus be ready to apply each individual step more intelligently.

2. Use either the exercises given or comparable exercises when you are ready to apply the material. The inclusion of *exercises* suggests certain similarities between developing a methodical approach to Biblical passages and developing a strong physique. Both are accomplished primarily through actual practice, and both are gradual and consequently demand patient perseverance. So just as a strong body cannot be realized by merely reading a discussion on the subject or taking a few easy lessons, it is not to be expected that a mere perusal of this book will produce methodicalness. If this discussion is to prove of real worth, it will be because it indicates certain lines of action which the reader may pursue, and by pursuing *teach himself* to be systematic in his Bible study. Such a process will take years if not an entire lifetime. For there is no convenient shortcut to methodical Bible study, just as there is no easy short-

cut to physical strength. However, though one's growth will not be rapid, if one adapts the forthcoming suggestions and actually engages in the mental and spiritual calisthenics they involve, one may be assured that under God one's efforts will bear increasing fruit.

3. Look up the illustrations in your Bible,[14] and make a serious attempt to discover wherein they illuminate the ideas in connection with which they are found. In fact, it would help to find your own illustrations for the various points.

4. During the first perusal of the manual, do not be too concerned about reading the notes, which are placed at the close of the various sections. The reason for this suggestion is to prevent frequent interruptions of the reader's train of thought when he is attempting to get a bird's-eye view of the whole. The notes should prove helpful during the subsequent readings of the manual, when one is in the process of applying its suggestions.

The purpose of the notes is threefold: first, to indicate bibliographical references; second, to provide explanatory material which experience has shown to be helpful but which would interrupt the trend and organization of the main discussion; and third, to serve as a system of cross references. The latter function is deemed essential for several reasons. For one thing, the notes thus become a partial substitute for an index, which is not included in the manual. Further, they serve as a means of correlating the various parts of the manual, thereby enabling the reader to see the integrality of methodical study; and they also contribute to the clarity of the discussion, since the different parts of the manual help to elucidate each other.

5. Utilize at least some of the bibliographical suggestions. This is necessary because the following presentation by no means exhausts the vast field of Bible study. In fact, there is not even space for a thorough demonstration of

methodical study in relation to a given passage, which would undoubtedly be beneficial. The discussion must of necessity be in the form of an outline guide which should be used in collaboration with other books in the field. Some of these books will be indicated in the course of the discussion and others in the bibliography.

6. Test the statements made for yourself. Just because they represent the conclusions of the writer's own inductive study, or at least so he hopes, and just because they represent his firm convictions, it does not follow that the reader is expected to accept them unquestioningly. On the contrary, the reader is urged to make his own inductive study. And if in so doing he arrives at conclusions which contradict those of this book, he has not only the privilege but the obligation to believe what he has found. These facts should be kept in mind throughout the discussion, even in connection with those statements which appear to be authoritarian. For there will be occasions when the reader will receive this impression, the main reason being that it is impossible within the scope of one volume to show all of the particulars upon which generalizations are based.

7. Practice suspended judgment. You are urged neither to accept nor reject statements immediately upon reading them. Give the ideas some time to take effect. If, for example, you are unable to see the purpose of certain suggestions, and if they appear to be superfluous or even ridiculous, leave room for the possibility that they may have a necessary function and that, given time, that function may become clear. Also have specific reasons for accepting or rejecting certain ideas. And even after you have formed conclusions, be willing to change them if and when new data come to light which necessitate such a change. These suggestions are true to the inductive approach.

8. Remember that this book attempts to present a compre-

hensive view of hermeneutics and is *primarily* designed for those who are training for a Christian profession. It does not follow that there can be no abbreviations. An average layman, for example, must have a simpler version if he is to study the Bible for himself. But it is supremely important to realize that one cannot begin with abbreviations; for it is impossible to abbreviate what does not already exist. Or, to put it another way, a more or less ideal concept is a requisite for a valid abbreviation.[15]

9. Be aware of the fact that repetition is *purposely* employed in this book as a necessary pedagogical device and in order to insure the thoroughness of its presentation. The writer has attempted to conceive of himself as a personal tutor of each one who reads this material. Therefore, his primary concern has not been to use the fewest possible words to describe methodical study, but rather to think in terms of effective communication. And repetition is one of the most effective means of imparting ideas.[16]

10. Do not be discouraged by the seeming complexity of the terminology and organization of this material. You will find that many of the terms used are simple though they may contain several syllables. You will also find that many of them are defined in the process of the discussion; your dictionary should help you with others. You will experience a sense of achievement as you develop the ability to use the various terms. As to the organization, what appears at first glance to be complex may in the last analysis bring about clarity of understanding. For the seeming complexity is not only due to the attempt to present a thoroughgoing exegetical approach, but also to the desire to anticipate the inevitable questions as to the relation of this idea or that practice to inductive Bible study. So the reader is urged not to be frustrated but rather to apply himself with the

confidence that what may be nebulous today may be lucid tomorrow. For the purpose of this discussion is not that everything be crystal clear the first time it is read, but that something be given the reader which will become clearer with application and into which he may grow for the remainder of his life. A *Quick*-magazine version of Bible study would be clearer in the immediate, but one has grave doubts as to its lasting qualities. The value of the forthcoming discussion lies more in its long-range effects than in its immediate effects.

11. Remember that mechanics are a necessary part of any worthwhile activity. Einstein became a great physicist because he first learned the laws of physics. Paderewski had to spend hours practicing finger exercises before he developed the ability to interpret the spirit of great composers. Neither of these men could have reached his position without so mastering the mechanics of his field that they became second nature to him and thus the means by which he could delve into the mysteries of the universe or capture the emotional quality of great music. Eliminate the mechanics of physics and piano playing, and you eliminate Einstein and Paderewski.

The same principle must be applied to Bible study. As much as one might like to avoid the mechanics of Bible study, one must realize that they cannot be eliminated. For there is no mystical or purely intuitive means of arriving at Scriptural truth. One cannot bypass the techniques of exegesis and expect to become a profound interpreter of the Bible any more than one can expect to become a great pianist without mastering the mechanics of fingering the keyboard. This is true even though to some students mechanics and the spirit appear to be irreconcilable because mechanics necessitate self-discipline and are at times tedious. One should be careful, however, not to equate the tedious with the unimportant, for such a mistake would be just as fatal

to a Bible student as for a pianist. Or, to put it positively, one should gladly discipline oneself to master the
mechanics, knowing that though the necessary road may
be hard, the joys to be found at the destination are well
worth the difficulties of the journey.

12. Methodicalness should not be made an end in itself.
This is a real danger, since the mechanics may loom so
large so as to hide their purpose. The development of
a methodical approach is merely the means of training
the mind to become a fit instrument for the operation
of God's Spirit. For since Biblical interpretation is
basically a rational process, the mind must function
properly if it is to be valid. But the mind's proper func-
tioning is not automatic. This is the burden of the following statement, which was made in connection with
A. E. Mander's *Logic for the Millions:*

> Thinking is skilled work. It is not true that we are
> naturally endowed with the ability to think clearly
> and logically—without learning how, or without
> practising . . . People with untrained minds
> should no more expect to think clearly and logically
> than people who have never learnt and never prac-
> tised can expect to find themselves good carpenters,
> golfers, . . . or pianists.

It follows, then, that the mind needs to be trained, or
it may become the means of negating God's Spirit. Methodicalness involves a description of how the Spirit
works through the mind and how one may cooperate
with the Spirit so that He may function freely.

Therefore, it should never be forgotten that the ultimate purpose of mechanics and of this manual is that
the reader may through their use in studying the Scriptures come to know the real author of the Scriptures,
the only true God, and Jesus Christ whom He has sent.
The writer has recorded the suggestions found on these

pages only because in his own experience their application has enabled him to realize a more intimate fellowship with God in Christ Jesus.

13. Avoid conceiving of this book as an attempt to dictate a precise and rigid formula for Bible study.[17] This suggestion is made for various reasons.

First, the very nature of the thought processes make it infeasible to coerce the mind into an inflexible pattern or an intellectual strait jacket. For example, one may indicate that certain steps should be taken before the interpretive phase of study begins. But at times one's thoughts will naturally move to interpretation, especially when the meaning of what is noted is obvious. Such elasticity is intrinsic to the mind and should not be violated.

Second, individual differences also make it impractical for one person to force upon others a stringent formula for Bible study. Now it is true that there are certain basic principles which may be laid down as essential and which cannot be transgressed if one's approach is to be sound. But when it comes to the precise application of these principles, each individual must be left to work out his own salvation.

Third, even in relation to the general pattern and concrete steps suggested one must make allowance for interplay. For the various phases of study are interdependent; the first step contributes to the second, and the second in turn contributes to the first. We shall have occasion to call attention to this principle frequently in the forthcoming discussion. Furthermore, none of the individual aspects of a study process is ever fully completed. Therefore, if it were necessary to finish the first step before moving to the second, the latter would never be reached.

For these and other reasons, the contents of the following pages should not be construed as an exact formula which is to be followed page for page every time one studies a given passage. Rather, *they primarily involve an analysis of Bible study which may be used as a basis for formulating a methodical approach to Biblical passages.* It is of supreme importance that this fact be understood if the following material is to be used properly. This manual attempts to dissect the study process to discover its component parts. It may therefore be likened to the exercises used to teach typing, which represent an analysis of the typing process. It is not expected that one will engage in all the typing exercises every time one types a letter. So it is not expected that every Bible study will be an exact replica of this book. On the contrary, the reader is urged to take the basic concepts involved in the forthcoming analysis and to use them as a foundation for building a methodical approach which will suit his own individual talents and needs.

14. Do not interpret the general pattern to be indicated as a single, final approach which may be executed conclusively at one sitting and need never be repeated. This suggestion is based on several facts.

First, the nature of the Scriptures makes it necessary. The Bible may be likened to an artesian well whose supply is inexhaustible, regardless of how much we drink of it. Consequently, no matter how valid a study process may be, it cannot be expected to consume the truth of a portion of Scripture in one application.

Second, our personal growth enables us to find more in the Scriptures tomorrow than we found today.

Third, at times the data discovered are inconclusive, and one finds it necessary to employ the hypothetical approach used by the scientist. In such instances one needs to test tentative conclusions to discover whether they are in keeping with all the available data. In fact, in certain cases one's interpretation may need to remain permanently tentative because the evidence is never conclusive.

Because of these facts it is erroneous to consider any approach as capable of a single and final application. On the contrary, the inductive pattern should be repeated in whole or in part, with each application enhanced as much as possible by what has transpired before.[18]

15. Do not allow questions to bog you down. You will find that many of them will be answered as you proceed, and that the unanswered ones will often diminish in significance.

16. Do not expect perfection. Any analysis will have its shortcomings; this is especially true of an analysis of mental processes. However, certain classifications will be used in spite of their obvious limitations because they have been found to contribute to the development of intelligent and effective study. An effort will be made to discuss some of the major problems which arise in this connection.[19]

NOTES

1. Webster, *Dictionary of Synonyms*, p. 545.
2. Dewey, J., "Method," *Cyclopedia of Education*, edited by Monroe, Volume IV, pp. 204-205.
3. This analogy between methodical Bible study and a cooking recipe should not be pressed too far. There are some important differences between the two which will be noted later. (Post, pp. 20-21.)
4. The writer is aware that these premises involve basic philosophical questions, and it should not be inferred from the brevity of the discussion that their importance is not realized. Nor should it be inferred that the position indicated cannot be substantiated. The lack of space makes a lengthy statement infeasible. If the reader is interested in exploring

these matters more fully, let him refer to the following
books: Eberhardt, C. R., *The Bible in the Making of Ministers;* Horne, H. H., *Psychological Principles of Education;*
and Kuist, H. T., *These Words Upon Thy Heart.*

5. See Adler, M. J., *How To Read a Book,* pp. 8-9.

6. Ibid., pp. 3-32. Also post, pp. 162-163. Note that the firsthand study of the Scriptures includes the use of such external helps as lexicons, grammars, concordances, historical
aids, etc. (Post, pp. 139ff.)

7. It is recognized that this represents a compromise with the
ideal, but it is done only because reality demands it. For a
fuller treatment of the reasons for making the vernacular
the primary basis for study, consult the pamphlet entitled
The Use of the Bible in the Forming of Men, which contains
the inaugural address of H. T. Kuist as the Charles T. Haley
Professor of Biblical Theology at Princeton Theological
Seminary. See also L. M. Sweet's *The Study of the English
Bible,* pp. 46-70. The place of the original in methodical
Bible study will be discussed later in this manual. (Post, pp.
128-129.)

8. Ferm, V., *Contemporary American Theology,* p. 216. The
fact that many universities study the Bible purely for its
literary values indicates the general acceptance of the Scriptures as outstanding literature.

9. Ibid., p. 214.

10. This statement implies that the basic unit of study is the
book, since the Bible is a library of books. There are some
notable exceptions, such as the four books of the Kings and
I and II Chronicles. However, even within these larger units
the book is in a real sense a structural entity.

11. Adapted from Bengel and taken from an article entitled
"The Kind of Study the Bible Teachers Training School
Stands For," *The Biblical Review,* January, 1916. The writer
is indebted to this article for many of the concepts used in
the discussion of basic premises.

12. Gilman, L., *Toscanini and Great Music,* p. 13.

13. These statements do not imply that one must approach the
Scriptures with a belief in their inspiration and authority
in order to receive anything from them. For if one needed

to believe that the Bible is God's Word before one could benefit from it, the principle of induction would be utterly negated. In fact, the validity of reason itself would be denied and there would arise the implication that one's choices must be made blindly. Faith would be transformed into credulity. For example, imagine a man who has lived on an island where he has not had the opportunity of hearing about the Scriptures. Two missionaries, one a Christian and one a Mohammedan, come to the island, and both insist that their particular books represent God's revelation to man. If the islander were forced to accept the proclamation of the missionaries before examining the books, he would have no basis for choosing between the Bible and the Koran. As a matter of fact, he could choose either with impunity because the basis of his choice would be the same in both cases. The Christian missionary would have no better appeal than the Mohammedan. On the other hand, if the islander were told, "Take these two books; examine them for yourself; read them and meditate on them; test their statements, and accept the one which best reveals God," then he would have a legitimate basis for making a decision. Moreover, we may rest assured that if the Scriptures are approached with an open mind and heart, because they do contain God's revelation to men in Jesus Christ, they will bear their own testimony through the operation of the Holy Spirit. The one who appeals to men on the latter basis has more faith in the Scriptures as God's Word than the one who asks men to accept their inspiration and authority before examining them. What is most essential in one's approach to the Scriptures, then, is a willingness to accept the truth once it is found. Therefore, the statements made under the category of reverence and similar statements apply to a more or less ideal situation, one in which the participants have at least a partial knowledge of the Scriptures. They express what is *ultimately* essential for a fuller understanding of the Scriptures, and not what is *initially* necessary for the discovery of any truth therein. This is in keeping with the inductive spirit.

14. It is suggested that either the American Revised Version or,

in the case of the New Testament, the Revised Standard Version be used as basic tools for study. These embody some of the latest findings of Biblical scholarship, are more suited to the vernacular of our day, are paragraphed, and are translations rather than paraphrases. These and other factors make them worthwhile textbooks. The American Revised Version may be obtained with wide margins for study notes.

15. The author is already planning a simplified version which may be used by laymen. It should be ready within the next few years.

16. See the law of repetition. (Post, p. 50.) Whatever success the author has had in teaching has been due to the fact that he has not been afraid to repeat ideas.

17. This is one of the points of difference between a cooking recipe and methodical study, for the former is much more rigid than the latter.

18. In this connection, consult L. M. Sweet's *The Study of the English Bible*, p. 20. Also note that it may be helpful to keep studies made on particular passages from time to time so that one may benefit from what has been done in the past; for it is often true that some discoveries previously made are not made in the following approaches to a passage. However, it is best to approach a passage without first looking at previous studies so as to avoid reducing the threshold of perception by prejudicing the mind. Then, when the later study is completed, it is well to compare it with previous studies so that present and past approaches may complement each other.

19. The author has learned that there is a difference between stating ideas and conveying them. He is therefore aware that though he has indicated in these introductory statements certain basic principles which will determine the course of the discussion, it does not follow that their full importance and implications will be immediately seen. There will be occasions, therefore, when some of these same ideas will be repeated or referred to, although this cannot be done at every point where they are relevant. The reader is urged to make a serious attempt to keep before him the basic

principles stressed in the introduction, for if he does he will
find that many of the questions which arise later will have
already been answered.

It should also be noted that some of the ideas found in
the introduction are out of place from the standpoint of
the inductive order, since they represent conclusions at the
outset of the study. However, this seeming violation of induction may be justified on these grounds: first, these conclusions represent the outgrowth of the author's own inductive study; second, they may be tested by the reader and
rejected if not inductively sound; and third, they are placed
in the introduction for pedagogical purposes.

CHAPTER ONE

Observation

CHAPTER ONE

Observation

SINCE THE BEGINNING of an inductive process involves noting the particulars, it is logical that the initial step of methodical Bible study should be that of observation.

I. DEFINITION AND PURPOSE OF OBSERVATION

Observation is "the act or faculty of . . . taking notice; the act or result of considering or marking attentively." [1] Dr. H. T. Kuist defines it as "the art of seeing things as they really are." He also suggests that it entails seeing "impartially, intensely, and fearlessly." [2]

It should be emphasized that truly to observe is to be mentally aware of what one sees. Observation transcends pure physical sight; it involves perception. Thus, for example, one may see a particular term used in the preceding sentence, namely, "perception." But unless one is conscious that this term has certain peculiar connotations and that an attempt must be made to discover them, one has not really observed its presence. Observation, then, is essentially *awareness*.

In view of its meaning, the general function of observation is to enable one to become *saturated* with the particulars of a passage so that one is thoroughly conscious of their existence and of the need for their explanation. Observation is the means by which the data of a passage become part of the mentality of the student. It supplies the raw materials upon which the mind may operate in the interpretive process.

II. REQUISITES OF OBSERVATION—SOME RELEVANT QUOTATIONS

A. The Will To Observe

This, then, is the bare chart of our coming journey; but everything depends upon the traveller's own eyes, and the disposition which he brings to this task of exploration. 'Seek and ye shall find,' is as true in history as in religion.[3]

Unwilled observation is soon satiated and goes to sleep. Willed observation, vision with excutive force behind it, is full of discernment, and is continually making discoveries which keep the mind alert and interested. Get a will behind the eye, and the eye becomes a searchlight, the familiar is made to disclose undreamed treasure.[4]

B. Exactness in Observation

Sir William Osler, the eminent physician, always sought to impress upon young medical students the importance of observing details. While stressing this point in a lecture before a student group he indicated a bottle on his desk. 'This bottle contains a sample for analysis,' he announced. 'It's possible by testing it to determine the disease from which the patient suffers.' Suiting actions to words, he dipped a finger into the fluid and then into his mouth. 'Now,' he continued, 'I am going to pass this bottle around. Each of you taste the contents

as I did and see if you can diagnose the case.' As the
bottle was passed from row to row, each student
gingerly poked his finger in and bravely sampled
the contents. Osler then retrieved the bottle. 'Gen-
tlemen,' he said, 'Now you will understand what I
mean when I speak about details. Had you been
observant you would have seen that I put my index
finger into the bottle but my middle finger into my
mouth.' [5]

C.   Persistence in Observation

Peering into the mists of gray
That shroud the surface of the bay,
Nothing I see except a veil
Of fog surrounding every sail.
Then suddenly against a cape
A vast and silent form takes shape,
A great ship lies against the shore
Where nothing has appeared before.

Who sees a truth must often gaze
Into a fog for many days;
It may seem very sure to him
Nothing is there but mist-clouds dim.
Then, suddenly, his eyes will see
A shape where nothing used to be.
Discoveries are missed each day
By men who turn too soon away.

Clarence Edward Flynn [6]

III. ANALYSIS OF OBSERVATION

The four main constituents of any Biblical passage are:
terms; the relations and interrelations between terms, or
structure; the general literary form or forms; and the atmosphere. These are therefore the concern of the observing eye.[7]

A. Observation of Terms

1. Definition of a Term

A term is a given word as it is used in a given context. It therefore has only one meaning, whereas the same word may have several. For instance, the word "trunk" may mean the main stem of a tree, the main body of anything, the proboscis of an elephant, or a box or chest. Though in all these cases the same word is used, "trunk" is one term when it signifies the main stem of a tree and another when it denotes the proboscis of an elephant.

2. Kinds of Terms

a. *Routine and Non-routine Terms*

The term is the basic component of literary communication, and as such every term should be noted by the careful observer. However, if the process of observation is to be efficient, especially from the standpoint of recording what one sees, a distinction needs to be made between those terms which are routine and those which are not routine.

In the former category may be placed those banal terms whose meaning is immediately obvious and which are not very significant for understanding a passage. For example, although occasionally an article will have unusual significance, most of the articles used belong in this category. It would therefore be a waste of time to make a careful record of the presence of every article in every sentence. On the other hand, there are terms which should be *especially* noted and should be recorded because they will require more particular consideration. These are the terms which are non-routine, and they fall into three classes: first, those which are difficult to understand; second, the crucial terms of a passage and those which, though not crucial, are nevertheless significant for understanding the statements of a passage; and third, those terms which otherwise express profound concepts. The terms "transfigured" and "appeared" in Mark 9:2, 4 might be considered non-routine.[8]

It should be emphasized that this distinction between routine and non-routine terms is not intended to discourage careful and thorough observation. Rather it is meant to develop discretion; and the more one's discretionary powers are developed, the more one will see terms which will need special consideration. Thus it will eventuate in more incisive and therefore more thorough observation.

b. *Literal and Figurative Terms*

Those terms are literal which should be interpreted according to the letter and which are meant to convey their primary or usual meaning. The term "tree" in Genesis 1:12 is literal. Figurative terms are those which are symbolic and which express a secondary idea distinct from their original meaning. The term "tree" in Romans 11:24 belongs in the figurative category.[9]

Frequently one will be able to determine whether a term is literal or figurative immediately upon seeing it. At times, however, this cannot be done until the second or interpretive step has been at least partially completed. In any case it is very important that one be aware of this distinction and that one use it properly if valid interpretation is to occur.[10]

3. Identity and Inflections of Terms

The various terms of a passage may be *identified* by the use of the following grammatical categories: nouns, pronouns,[11] verbs, adjectives, adverbs, prepositions, conjunctions, interjections, and articles. The observer should be able to utilize these categories and he should be aware of their functions.

To the ability to identify terms should be added the ability to note their *inflections*. An inflection is a change of form undergone by terms to indicate their case, gender, number, tense, person, mood, voice, etc. Inflections are especially significant in relation to nouns, pronouns, verbs, and adjectives.[12]

Exercise

Observe every term of Mark 10:13-52 and Romans 6. Try to determine whether each term is routine or non-routine, literal or figurative. Note any significant inflections. Attempt to indicate why the non-routine terms will need special consideration.

B. Observation of Relations and Interrelations Between Terms—Structure

1. Definition of Structure and Various Structural Units

As we have already noted, the basic component of literary expression is the term. But in order to communicate ideas, terms must be related and interrelated in accordance with certain mental, linguistic, and literary patterns. These relations form what is known as "structure." Thus in a *general* sense structure involves all of the relations and interrelations which bind terms into a literary unit, from the minutest to the broadest, from the least significant to the most significant. In a more *restricted* sense "structure" may be used to denote the framework or skeleton of a passage, that is, its more essential relations. "Structure" will be used in both the general and restricted senses in the forthcoming discussion.[13]

The various structural units may be defined as follows:

phrase —   a group of two or more terms constituting a partial unit of thought and expression

clause —   a group of terms, including a subject and verb and sometimes one or more phrases, constituting a partial (or whole) unit of thought and expression sentence — one or more clauses constituting a unit of thought and expression

paragraph — a group of sentences constituting a unit of thought and expression [14]

segment — a group of paragraphs constituting a unit of thought and expression

subsection — a group of segments constituting a unit of thought and expression [15]

section — a group of subsections (or segments) constituting a unit of thought and expression

division — a group of sections constituting a unit of thought and expression

book — a group of divisions constituting a unit of thought and expression

2. Importance of Structure

In one of his books, Henry O. Taylor states: ". . . art is not spontaneous, but carefully intended; no babbling of a child, but a mutual fitting of form and content, in which efficient unison the artist's intellect has worked." [16] One of the chief aspects of the "form" to which Taylor refers is literary structure. By the preceding statement Taylor thus emphasizes the great importance of structure for the accomplishment of the artist's purpose, as well as the importance of the awareness of structure on the part of the observer if he is to comprehend this purpose. There is no doubt, then, that the discovery of structure is "one of the crucial points where conditions of growth have to be carefully maintained and fostered." [17] The reader is therefore urged to aim at becoming *structure-conscious,* for if he does so he will find many passages unfolding before his eyes which he otherwise could not understand.

3. Types of Structure

Any given passage of Biblical literature may contain various kinds of structural factors. These may be classified in terms of two main categories: first, the comparative ease of their discovery, and second, their relative importance.

a. *Surface and Subsurface Structure*

There are some structural elements which are explicit and are therefore immediately apparent to the trained observer. We shall refer to these as "surface structure," since, as the name implies, they lie on the exterior of a passage. Romans 1:18-32 affords an excellent example of surface structure, for the "therefore" of 1:24 immediately indicates that the passage is constructed in terms of cause and effect.

On the other hand, some structural factors are more implicit and consequently may not be observed as readily as those which are expressed. These will be referred to as "subsurface structure." The contrasts implied between David and Amnon in II Samuel 11-13 and between Judah and Joseph in Genesis 38-39 are good illustrations of this kind of structure.

Certain facts should be noted in connection with the distinction between surface and subsurface structure.

First, it does not necessarily involve the difference between the less profound and the more profound, but rather is primarily concerned with the more obvious and the less obvious.

Second, not all passages have both explicit and implicit structure. In the study of some units, if one observes their surface structure and delves thoroughly into its meaning, one will arrive at the author's message. However, the observer should always be on the lookout for those structural elements which lie on the interior of a passage. He should never conclude that because he has noted some exterior relations, he has noted the complete framework of the passage.

Third, the discovery of subsurface structure must frequently await at least partial completion of the interpretive step. Therefore, it is the noting of surface structure which is primarily involved in observation.[18]

Finally, both surface and subsurface structure are effected by the same laws of composition.

b. Primary and Secondary Structure

A further differentiation should be made on the basis of the relative importance of structural elements within a given passage. It should be recognized that some connections are primary and that others are secondary or subordinate. In certain instances one may need to await at least a partial completion of interpretation to make such a distinction, but at least the observer should be aware of it and should attempt to utilize it insofar as is possible in the initial step of study. For it is important that primary emphasis be given to primary relations, and that secondary structural elements be conceived as subservient to these primary relations if the author's stress is to be ascertained.

4. Specific Laws of Structure

The structural laws about to be set forth indicate the concrete means used by any artist in arranging his work, whether he be a musician, a painter, or an author. In all these cases the means are essentially one. For what is art but the expression of the mind of the artist; and since mind is one, all the arts are one. All one needs to do, therefore, is to observe the composition of various artistic productions and by so doing discover the means used by artists in effecting the structural unity of their works. As a result of such an inductive approach, one will have valid grounds for looking for these laws in Scriptural literature, which is great art, and using them for its interpretation.

Frequently the forthcoming structural relations are conceived as convenient inventions which are imposed upon Biblical literature in order to prove a point. It should therefore be crystal clear at the outset that the laws to be stated are laws of logic; they reflect the mental processes of men as they think and as they express themselves in whatever medium they may choose to employ. Therefore, *the observer does not apply them to a work of art; he simply discovers them* and thereby ascertains the message of the artist. For the same relations which provide the universal means of communication also afford the universal avenues for interpretation.[19]

> a. *Structural Relations Within Phrases and Clauses, Between Clauses, and Between Sentences—Within Paragraphs*

It would seem logical to consider the sentence as the fundamental structural unit and therefore to limit our discussion at this point to an examination of the relations within sentences. However, since sentences are frequently determined by rather arbitrary means, especially in translating the Scriptural text, and since the relations between clauses within a sentence are often identical to those between sentences, *the paragraph will be used as the basic structural unit rather than the sentence.* The relations between sentences will therefore be surveyed together with the relations within sentences.[20]

Structure as related to clauses and sentences is called "syntax." Webster defines "syntax" as ". . . the due arrangement of word forms to show their mutual relations in a sentence." [21] We will now enumerate these syntactical relations in conjunction with the similar relations which exist between sentences. Together they will be termed "paragraphical relations." The following list will not be exhaustive but will rather indicate some of the more important connections.

(1) **Presentation of Paragraphical Relations**

    (a) The relation of subject to verb. The subject may be a noun, pronoun, infinitive, gerund, or dependent clause.

    (b) The relation of verb to predicate, which may involve a direct object, an indirect object, a predicate noun, a predicate adjective or adjectival clause, or an adverb or adverbial clause.

    (c) The relation of modifier to modified includes adjectives, participles, adverbs, articles, demonstrative pronouns, prepositional phrases, and adjectival and adverbial clauses.

    (d) The relation of preposition to object.

    (e) The relation of pronoun to antecedent.

    (f) The relation of independent (coordinate) clauses to each other in compound sentences and the relation of dependent (subordinate) and independent clauses in complex sentences.[22] Some of the various kinds of independent and dependent clauses may be described by the following names: relative, subordinate causal, local, subordinate comparative, temporal, purpose, result, conditional, concessive, substantival, indirect discourse, coordinate causal, and coordinate comparative.[23]

    The relations between the different types of clauses are indicated for the most part by coordinate and subordinate connectives, the chief of which will now be mentioned. Some of them will be expressed by prepositional phrases which serve as connectives. They will be placed under four classes and Biblical references will be given for them.[24] The categories are as follows: temporal or chronological, local or geographical, logical, and emphatic.

Temporal or Chronological connectives
   after (Revelation 11:11)
   as (Acts 16:16)
   before (John 8:58)
   now (Luke 16:25)
   then (I Corinthians 15:6)
   until (Mark 14:25)
   when (John 11:31)
   while (Mark 14:43)
Local or Geographical connectives
   where (Hebrews 6:20) [25]
Logical connectives
   Reason—because (Romans 1:25)
      for (Romans 1:11)
      since (Romans 1:28)
   Result—so (Romans 9:16)
      then (Galatians 2:21)
      therefore (I Corinthians 10:12)
      thus (I Corinthians 8:12)
   Purpose—in order that (Romans 4:16)
      so that (Romans 5:21)
   Contrast—although (Romans 1:21)
      but (Romans 2:8)
      much more (Romans 5:15)
      nevertheless (I Corinthians 10:5)
      otherwise (I Corinthians 14:16)
      yet (Romans 5:14)
   Comparison—also (II Corinthians 1:11)
      as (Romans 9:25)
      as—so (Romans 5:18)
      just as—so (Romans 11:30-31)
      likewise (Romans 1:27)
      so also (Romans 4:6)
   Series of Facts [26]—and (Romans 2:19)
      first of all (I Timothy 2:1)
      last of all (I Corinthians 15:8)

or (II Corinthians 6:15)
Condition—if (Romans 2:19)
Emphatic connectives
indeed (Romans 9:25)
only (I Corinthians 8:9) [27]

Several facts should be noted in regard to these relations between clauses and sentences.

First, the four categories employed are not mutually exclusive. For example, a temporal connective may also imply a logical relation. Moreover, some of the same connectives may be found in more than one category.

Second, many of these same relations are operative within clauses as well as between clauses. The use of similes and metaphors, for instance, involves comparison. For an excellent illustration of this see the parables of Matthew 13.

Third, sometimes clauses and sentences are related implicitly rather than explicitly. Therefore, the mere absence of expressed connections does not mean that they are unrelated. At times one may need to infer relations from a study of the thoughts expressed or from the comparative positions of the clauses or sentences in question. Note, for example, Hebrews 8:5. [28]

(2) Illustrations of Paragraphical Relations

In order to clarify the significance of the various paragraphical relations, they will now be illustrated in two ways: first, by investigating the relations within a sentence taken from a logical type of literature, the Epistle to the Romans; and second, by noting some of the main connections in a paragraph taken from a narrative type of literature, the Gospel by Mark.

(a) Relations in Romans 1:18

Romans 1:18 reads: ". . . the wrath of God is revealed from heaven against all ungodliness and wickedness of men who by their wickedness suppress the truth." The subject of the sentence is "wrath." The article "the" and the prepositional phrase "of God" both modify "wrath," the latter denoting the possessor of the wrath and therefore its source. The main verb of the sentence is the verb "is revealed." The prepositional phrases "from heaven" and "against all ungodliness and wickedness" both modify the verb, the former further indicating the source and the latter the objects of the action expressed by the verb, as well as the reason for that action. The adjective "all" modifies the nouns "ungodliness" and "wickedness," which are related by the conjunction "and." The prepositional phrase "of men" also modifies the same two nouns and indicates, together with the adjectival, dependent, relative clause "who by their wickedness suppress the truth," the possessors of the qualities denoted by the nouns. In the dependent clause the relative pronoun "who" is the subject, the main verb is "suppress," and the direct object is the noun "truth." "Truth" is qualified by the definite article "the." The prepositional phrase "by their wickedness" modifies the verb "suppress," showing the means by which the action of the verb is realized as well as its cause. The entire clause indicates the expression of "ungodliness and wickedness" and therefore denotes the cause for the revelation of the wrath of God.[29]

(b) Relations in Mark 9:2-8

    1) "Jesus took with him Peter and James and John." (v. 2)—Peter, James, and John are the direct objects of the verb "took." Jesus took three disciples with him instead of the twelve, and he took these particular three.[30]

    2) "apart by themselves" (v. 2)—This is a good

example of a pleonasm. The prepositional phrase "by themselves" strengthens the adverb "apart." They both modify the verb "led." The question arises as to whether the author had any specific purpose in so utilizing the principle of redundancy.

3) "before them" (v. 2)—This prepositional phrase modifies the verb "transfigured" and suggests the place of the transfiguration, that is, in their presence. The antecedent of the pronoun "them" is the group of three disciples.

4) "and his garments became glistening, intensely white, as no fuller on earth could bleach them." (v. 3)—The predicate participle "glistening" modifies the subject "garments." The adverb "intensely" modifies the adjective "white" and both terms define the noun "garments." The "as" is a comparative connective introducing a comparative subordinate clause. The comparison is between the glistening, intensely white quality of Jesus' garments and the clause "no fuller on earth could bleach them." In effect, "no" modifies the entire clause and not only its subject. The prepositional phrase "on earth" qualifies the subject "fuller" and implies that the event is the work of a "heavenly fuller."

5) "And there appeared to them Elijah with Moses" (v. 4)—The prepositional phrase "to them" is an indirect object of the verb "appeared" and suggests to whom the appearance was made. Since the pronoun "them" is plural, it indicates that the disciples were aware of the appearance of Elijah with Moses. In the expression "Elijah with Moses," Elijah is mentioned first although chronologically Moses

preceded him. The preposition "with" is used to relate Elijah and Moses instead of other possible connectives.

6) "and they were talking to Jesus" (v. 4)—Elijah and Moses are the antecedents of the pronoun "they," thus indicating that they were both speaking to Jesus. "To Jesus" is the indirect object of "talking." Elijah and Moses were talking to Jesus, not to the disciples.

7) "And Peter said to Jesus, 'Master, it is well that we are here: let us make three booths, one for you and one for Moses and one for Elijah.'" (v. 5)—The adverbial subordinate clause "that we are here" modifies the main clause "it is well" and especially the predicate adjective "well." The subject of the statement "let us make three booths" is in the first person and it is plural. The object of the verb "make" is "booths," which, interestingly enough, is modified by the adjective "three." The apposition "one for you and one for Moses and one for Elijah" qualifies the "three booths," indicating for whom they should be built. In this statement Moses is mentioned before Elijah.

8) "For he did not know what to say, for they were exceedingly afraid." (v. 6)—Here are two coordinate causal clauses explaining the reasons for the facts stated. The first clause, "For he did not know what to say," gives the cause for the statement of Peter in v. 5, especially the latter part concerning the booths. The second clause, "for they were exceedingly afraid," explains the reason for the first clause of v. 6, that is, for Peter's not knowing what to say. The subject of the second clause is plural, whereas the subject of the first is singular.

Note also the adverb "exceedingly," which modifies the predicate adjective "afraid."

9) "And a cloud overshadowed them, and a voice came out of the cloud, 'This is my beloved Son; listen to him.'" (v. 7)—The pronoun "them" is the direct object of the verb "overshadowed." A question arises as to the antecedent of this pronoun. The voice came out of the same cloud which overshadowed them. The statement made by the voice is given, although the voice is not identified, since it is preceded by the indefinite article "a." The subject of the statement is the demonstrative pronoun "this," which refers to Jesus. Both the pronoun "my" and the adjective "beloved" qualify the predicate noun "Son." The exhortation "listen to him" follows the statement of the fact, "This is my beloved Son." A relation is probably implied by this order. The factual statement seems to be the cause, the exhortation the effect: "Because this is my beloved Son, listen to him."

10) "And suddenly looking around they no longer saw any one with them but Jesus only." (v. 8) —The adverb "suddenly" may modify either the participle "looking" or the verb "saw," or both. The subject of the sentence is the pronoun "they," referring to the disciples. Note the connective "but" and the relation it suggests between "any one" and Jesus. Note also the succession of terms emphasizing the same factor: "no longer," "any one," "but," "only."

Here are some facts which should be kept in mind regarding this illustration from Mark 9.

First, the preceding observations are made solely on the

basis of the English translation in order to demonstrate the firsthand study of the vernacular.

Second, there is room for a difference of opinion as to the analysis of some of the relations. This fact, however, is not of great consequence. It is the process which is of primary importance.

Third, this illustration is not meant to be duplicated in the observation of the paragraphical relations of every passage. It rather represents an analysis which demonstrates how grammatical relations are utilized to convey facts and how an awareness of them may lead to an awareness of the facts they communicate.

Fourth, not all of the relations indicated are of great significance. Nor should one always be interested in noting only those things which seem to have immediate and outstanding import. For often an observation which seems to lack much significance at first glance becomes very important in the long run. *The process of observation should generally resemble the absorbing process of the sponge when it is exposed to a liquid.*[31] The observer should not place limitations on his perception which will hinder his receptivity. It is true that the observational procedure should be discriminating in certain ways, as was suggested in the discussion of routine and non-routine terms; but no hindrances should be imposed on the eyes which will hamper thorough observation.

Fifth, in some instances, such as the final statement under 4), the writer indulged slightly in the second step of the inductive process, namely, interpretation. This was done primarily to indicate the significance of some of the observations. Apart from this it should be remembered that at times observation and interpretation are almost inseparable. As was noted heretofore, there is often an interplay between the different steps which cannot and should not be totally avoided.[32] *Nevertheless, it is important that one always be able to distinguish between the various steps when called*

upon to do so. For if there is ever a blurring of the process
to the extent that the various phases of study become indis-
tinguishable, then eisegesis will inevitably result.

If one is able to note the paragraphical relations set forth
in the preceding pages, one's chances for thorough observation and consequently for accurate and incisive interpretation will be greatly enhanced. This does not imply that at
all times one must make a detailed analysis of these relations. For example, one may observe the fact that "Jesus
took with him Peter and James and John" without being
conscious that "Jesus" is the subject of the clause, that the
verb is "took," and that the prepositional phrase "with him"
modifies the verb, and that "Peter," "James," and "John"
are the direct objects of the verb, connected to each other by
the conjunction "and." Nevertheless, one should always be
aware that such relations are operative within clauses and
sentences, and that it is through them that facts and their
relations to one another are communicated. Furthermore,
one should be capable of making a minute analysis when
necessary; for there will arise occasions, especially in the
study of the argumentative type of literature, when such a
conscious analysis is imperative for proper observation. This
is true, for example, in one's observation of Romans 1:1-7.

Exercise

Observe the paragraphical connections in several chapters
of the epistles of the New Testament. Note especially the
relations indicated by connectives, prepositional phrases,
and dependent clauses. Look also for those relations which
are implicit rather than explicit. Classify the connections
you find in view of the preceding discussion. Attempt to indicate the significance of your discoveries for interpretation.

b. *Structural Relations Between Paragraphs, Segments, Subsections, Sections, Divisions, and Books*

The preceding pages have been concerned with those relations which are grammatical in nature. We now move to those broader structural elements which are more *literary* than purely grammatical. This is not meant to imply that the two are mutually exclusive; for it will be found that many of the paragraphical or grammatical relations, such as contrast and comparison, will be utilized to make possible literary structure. Moreover, some of the broader structural relations will be indicated by grammatical means, such as the "therefore" of Romans 12:1. However, in a real sense literary structure transcends grammatical structure; for it is possible to compose sentences in paragraph form without at the same time arranging a work with literary unity.[33]

There follows a list of the main literary relations which operate to make possible the framework of Biblical books together with definitions and illustrations of them. Some of the connections already mentioned will be restated because of their significance for literary structure and in order further to elucidate them.

(1) Comparison—the association of like things. The unity of Hebrews 5:1-10 is based on the use of this law. Note the "so also" in v. 5.

(2) Contrast—the association of opposites. Romans 4 utilizes contrast.

(3) Repetition—the reiteration of the *same* terms, phrases, clauses, etc. In Leviticus the term "holy" is repeated many times.

(4) Continuity—the repeated use of *similar* terms, phrases, clauses, etc. In the law of repetition the recurring factors are exactly the same, whereas in continuity they are merely more or less alike. The series of parables in Luke 15 is an example of the latter.

(5) Continuation—the extended treatment of a particular aspect; the carrying through to its completion of an idea or series of events. This law is sometimes related to that of continuity, but it involves *extension* rather

than recurrence. One of the relations between Genesis 13-14 and Genesis 18-19 is that of continuation.[34]

(6) Climax—the arrangement of material in such a way as to progress from the lesser to the greater and ultimately to the greatest. The book of Exodus is arranged climactically, with the high point coming in 40:34-35.

(7) Cruciality—the utilization of the principle of the pivot. The subject matter is arranged so that it turns around or upon some one factor. II Samuel uses the law of cruciality, with chapters 11-12 forming the pivotal point which changes the direction of the history recorded there.

(8) Interchange—the exchanging or alternation of certain elements. Interchange is often employed to strengthen contrasts or comparisons. The opening chapters of I Samuel contain alternating contrasts between Hannah and her son Samuel, and Eli and his sons. Luke also uses interchange in chapters 1-2.

(9) Particularization and Generalization—the movement from the general to the particular, and from the particular to the general. Matthew 6:1-18 is an example of particularization, and James 2 an example of generalization.

(10) Causation and Substantiation—the progression from cause to effect and from effect to cause. Romans 1:18-32 is an excellent illustration of causation, and Romans 8:18-30 of substantiation.

(11) Instrumentation—the setting forth of the means to an end as well as the end itself. Instrumentation thus involves the factor of purpose. The Gospel by John, in view of the author's statement in 20:30-31, exemplifies this law. The signs recorded in the book are a means to an end, namely, belief in Jesus as the Christ, the Son of God, in order to make possible eternal life.

In connection with this law, one should be aware that simply because one aspect of a passage is labeled "means," it does not follow that it is less significant than that labeled "end." Often instruments are no less dispensable than their purposes. Also, it should be noted that there is a similarity between the law of instrumentation and the preceding law, since means often have a causal relation to their purpose.

(12) Explanation or Analysis—the presentation of an idea or event followed by its interpretation. Mark 4 contains an example of this law. It is closely related to particularization.

(13) Preparation or Introduction—the inclusion of the background or setting for events or ideas. Thereby the reader is prepared to understand that which follows by that which precedes. This kind of composition is frequently utilized in narrative literature. For example, Genesis 2:4-25 provides the situation in which the events of Genesis 3 occur.

(14) Summarization—the employment of an abridgement or compendium either preceding or following a unit of material. Joshua 12 exemplifies this kind of structure.

(15) Interrogation—the employment of a question or problem followed by its answer. Romans 6-7 affords an illustration of this type of arrangement.

(16) Harmony—the effecting of unity by means of agreement. Included in this concept is the *law of consistency*. The law of harmony is not so much a law of composition as a law of truth. However, since truth is communicated through structural relations, the two are ultimately inseparable. Illustrations of this law are found in the harmony between the disease and its remedy and the promise and its fulfilment. See, for example, the agreement between Romans 1:18-3:20 and Romans 3:21ff.[35]

The following facts should be remembered concerning these structural relations.

First, it should be noted that these laws are closely inter-related. For instance, contrast is sometimes effected through interchange; repetition and continuity are two forms of the same basic law; particularization and summarization have much in common with each other. It is evident, then, that there is no clear-cut line of distinction between them. In fact, they are often used in combination with one another.

Second, because structural laws are often used in combinations, it will sometimes be difficult to ascertain which law or laws are primary and which are subordinate in a given passage. In some cases a decision in this matter will depend on the makeup of the unit itself. It should also be remembered that there are some relations which by their very nature are subservient to others. For example, the law of interchange is inherently subordinate, since something must be interchanged, and what is interchanged is more basic than the interchange itself. Interchange is therefore employed for the purpose of strengthening some other structural relation, such as contrast, comparison, or causation.

Third, attention should be called to the fact that the preceding list is not all inclusive. For the types of arrangement used in some passages are difficult to categorize. In addition, there are variations of the relations which have been mentioned. But most of the major laws are contained in the preceding list, and the ability to observe them will result in the ability to note those not mentioned.

Fourth, the descriptive terms used to indicate the different relations may be varied, for in some instances other terms are more accurate and more expressive. The factors which determine how one shall refer to the relations of a certain passage are the individual tastes of the observer and the nature of the unit being studied. For example, causation may be expressed by the term "motivation" in the analysis of John 13:1ff. or by the term "purpose" in the analysis of Jude

3ff. The important thing is not the uniformity of nomenclature in describing the various relations, but an awareness
of specific and well-defined laws of structure and the attempt
to analyze passages in terms of them. For vagueness is fatal
to structural observation.

Fifth, differences of opinion frequently arise in connection with structural analysis. When this occurs, one may be
tempted to conclude that the process being suggested is subjective and therefore not dependable. Now it is true that
subjective elements may enter into it and be the cause for
differences of opinion. However, merely because this may
happen, it does not follow that the process itself should be
discarded. For every good thing has its dangers, because
every good thing may be misused. The doctrine of justification by faith through grace, for instance, has been interpreted so as to condone sin.[36] And yet we do not discard
justification by faith because of this; rather we make an
effort to interpret it properly and thus avoid the danger of
license. So in relation to Bible study, the rational approach
to such a problem is to erect safeguards which will insure
insofar as possible that one's conclusions will be based on the
concrete data of the passage being studied and not on personal prejudices or wishful thinking. It also helps to realize
that differences of opinion often arise because various people
see varying facets of the same truth. George Denny, moder-
ator of "The Town Meeting of the Air," demonstrates this
fact by the use of a ball, one half of which is black and the
other half white. Holding the black side toward the audience
so that the white half cannot be seen, he asks, "What color
is this ball?" The audience replies, "Black." Then, turning
the ball around, Mr. Denny retorts, "No. It is white." Furthermore, it should be remembered that at times the evidence for varying possibilities is evenly distributed, and differences will arise when one places more emphasis on certain
data whereas another stresses the data which support a differing view. To summarize, the task of re-creating the minds

and purposes of authors who wrote hundreds of years ago is a very complex one, and at times one cannot be sure that one has succeeded. However, one ought to make the attempt to interpret them in spite of the probability of error, because there are valid bases for so doing and one cannot afford to miss the values which may be derived from their writings.[37]

5. Materials for Effecting Structure

a. *Materials Described*

The *structure* of a passage may be likened to the framework of a building. The *structural relations* which are used to construct a passage, such as contrast and comparison, correspond to the architectural concepts which are expressed by a building's framework. For instance, if the building is to be of Gothic design, then the individual parts of its skeleton will be related to each other in a certain manner, whereas the parts of its skeleton would be arranged differently if it were constructed on the basis of a modern design. The *materials* for effecting the structure of a passage may be compared with the steel or concrete used to execute a certain architectural concept in the construction of a building.

To be more specific, a literary unit cannot be constructed without the stuff from which literature is made. For example, an author cannot utilize the law of contrast to arrange a passage unless he has two things which he may contrast. That which he uses in the contrast is what has been termed the "material" for effecting structure. The various materials which may be used will now be enumerated and described.

(1) Biographical Material—*Persons* are often used to make possible structural relations. In Genesis 12-50, which is constructed from biographical materials, Abraham

is contrasted to Lot, Jacob to Esau, and Joseph to his brothers.

(2) Historical Material—*Events* are frequently employed as the "mortar and bricks" from which to construct passages. (Numbers)

(3) Chronological Material—The *time* element may be employed to effect literary structure. (Gospel by John)

(4) Geographical Material—*Places* sometimes serve as the stuff from which to build literary passages. (Exodus)

(5) Ideological or Logical Material—*Ideas* are used on many occasions to realize structural relations. (Romans)

The following facts should be noted regarding the materials for effecting structure.

First, there are no clear-cut lines of demarcation between them. In the process of using two persons to effect a comparison, one may also employ events; for people are the actors who make possible events, and one thinks of people in terms of what they do. And since events occur in time and at particular places, one cannot ultimately separate the chronological and the geographical from the biographical and the historical. Therefore, in analyzing a passage one should not think of one means to the exclusion of the others, but rather in terms of the means which is primary.

Second, the materials by which structural relations are executed may be at the same time the reasons for the use of structural relations. For instance, the desire to express certain ideas (ideological material) may cause an author to use particular laws of arrangement, such as repetition or instrumentation. So that by describing the factors listed above as materials, we are not thereby implying that they are only materials. We are rather calling attention to one of their functions, the function which is of primary interest at this juncture of our study.

b. *Materials Illustrated*

In order to clarify further the relationship between the laws of composition and the materials used to execute them, there follows a list of the various relations involved in literary structure together with some examples of how they are realized by the use of the materials heretofore discussed.

(1) Comparison
   Biographical—I Samuel 13-31, I Kings 17-II Kings 13
   Historical—Genesis 12, 20, and 26
   Ideological—John 13:1-35, Romans 5:12-21

(2) Contrast
   Biographical—I Samuel 13-31, John 18-19
   Chronological—Exodus 19-Numbers 10 and Numbers 11ff.
   Geographical—Exodus 1-12:40 and 12:41ff.
   Historical—Deuteronomy 1-3, Joshua 7-8, Mark 9:1-29
   Ideological—Deuteronomy 27-30, Isaiah 2-4, 10:5-12:6, 40-44, Micah 1-5, Matthew 5:17-48, Jude

(3) Repetition
   Historical—Joshua 24:2-13, Judges
   Ideological—Deuteronomy 5-11, Joshua 1, Habakkuk 2, Matthew 23, I Corinthians 13

(4) Continuity
   Chronological—John
   Historical—Genesis 37-50, Exodus 7-13, Mark 2:1-3:6, Mark 4:35-5:43
   Ideological—Isaiah 13-23, Mark 4:1-34, I Timothy 4:6-6:2, Revelation 6, 8-9, 16

(5) Continuation
   Biographical—Numbers 22-24, Jonah
   Geographical—Deuteronomy

(6) Climax
   Historical—Exodus, Mark 1:14-45
   Ideological—Ecclesiastes

(7) Cruciality
Biographical—II Samuel 11
Geographical—Exodus 12
Historical—Exodus 5:1-6:8

(8) Interchange
Biographical—I Samuel 1-12
Ideological—Hosea 1-3, Nahum 1, I John

(9) Particularization and Generalization
Particularization
Ideological—Deuteronomy 5-26, Isaiah 5, 40, Matthew 5:17-48, Romans 12:1-15:13, I Corinthians 1:10-4:21, Hebrews 11
Generalization
Historical—Acts
Ideological—James 2

(10) Causation and Substantiation
Causation
Historical—Deuteronomy 1-4, Isaiah 7, Acts 1-2
Ideological—Ephesians 1-3 and 4-6
Substantiation
Ideological—Habakkuk 2, Hebrews 1:4-2:18

(11) Instrumentation
Ideological—Romans 5:1-11

(12) Explanation or Analysis
Historical—Mark 3, 11
Ideological—John 5

(13) Preparation or Introduction
Historical—Genesis 2:4-25 and 3, Exodus 2-4 and 5:1-6:8, 25-34 and 35-40, Joshua 1 and 2ff., Isaiah 7
Ideological—Romans 1:18-3:20 and 3:21ff.

(14) Summarization
Biographical—Genesis 45
Historical—Joshua 12, 23-24, II Kings 17
Ideological—Romans 1:16-17, 3:21-31

(15) Interrogation
     Historical—Genesis 15, Exodus 5:1-6:8, Mark 11:27-
        12:37, 13, John 6, 13:36-14:24
     Ideological—Habakkuk, Romans 3:1-8, 6-7, 9-11
(16) Harmony
     Historical—Genesis 28-35
     Ideological—Ephesians 1-3 and 4-6

Since the laws of composition are realized by the use of
these materials, as demonstrated by the preceding list, it is
helpful to use such descriptive expressions as "biographical
comparison" or "logical contrast" or "historical repetition"
to indicate *precisely* the different structural relations.[38]

6. Selectivity and Structure

a. *Meaning and Importance of Selectivity*

Goethe once said, "The artist is known by selection."
Someone else has observed that much had to be excluded
from the Biblical record in order for some to be included.
Since those who wrote Scriptural literature were artists in
the truest sense, both of the preceding statements imply the
same thing, namely, that *purposive selectivity characterizes
the books of the Bible.* In other words, Biblical authors had
definite purposes which motivated their writings, and they
chose their materials and utilized them in such a way so as
best to accomplish their purposes.

The factor of selectivity, then, is basic to the work of
Scriptural writers. However, it is also important for the work
of the observer. For he is ultimately searching for the author's purpose, which is disclosed on the one hand by what
the author chooses to implement it, and on the other by
what he chooses not to use. Consequently, an awareness of
the principle of purposive selection is just as significant for
the observer as it is for the author in the first place.

b. *Relation of Selectivity to Structure*

The process of selectivity on the part of an author is closely associated with literary structure. An author often chooses certain ideas or events because they bear certain connections to other ideas and events, relations whose employment will contribute to the realization of his objective. In the selection of those things which should be included in his book, the writer asks himself, either consciously or unconsciously, "How are these events or ideas related to other events or ideas? Are these relations conducive to the accomplishment of my purpose in writing this particular piece of literature?" An author's selection, then, is founded on an awareness and utilization of structural relations.

Because in an author's mind selectivity and structure are closely related, the recognition of the principle of selectivity on the part of the observer eventuates in his discovery of structural relations. For when one is aware of purposive selection, one will want to find the reasons for it; and to do so one must ask such questions as these: "What relation is there between this event or idea and the other events or ideas which surround it which caused the author to include it? How does its inclusion contribute to the framework of the whole?" By answering such questions, the observer is led to perceive the structure of a unit and consequently its message.

Thus the observer's utilization of the principle of selectivity becomes a helpful means of discovering structural relations. For certain relations led to an author's selection in the first place; therefore, an examination of his selection will in turn lead to a discovery of those same relations. For example, one of the reasons why the writer or compiler of Genesis chose to include the event of 12:10-20 must have been its relation to the events which surround it. When one attempts to find what some of those relations could be, one notes two among others: a contrast between an act of faith in 12:1-9

and an act of unbelief in 12:10-20, and the relation of causation in that God's protection of Abraham in verses 10-20 is
a fulfilment of the promise made to Abraham in verses 1-9.
In this manner the use of the principle of selectivity becomes a valuable avenue for uncovering structural laws and
through them the author's purpose.[39]

c. Kinds of Selectivity

(1) Quantitative or Proportionate Selectivity

This type of selection utilizes the element of mass or
quantity. It entails the choice of a series of similar events or
ideas whose sheer weight impresses certain facts on the reader's mind. Such selectivity is usually based on the laws of
repetition and continuity.

The presence and importance of quantitative selectivity
are often discovered by the application of the law of proportion, which involves the principle that an author devotes the
greatest quantity of material proportionately to that which
he feels is most significant and most helpful in conveying his
message. Consequently, the observer often becomes aware of
quantitative selectivity by determining the ratio between the
amount of material concerned with certain facts and the
time span covered by those facts, and by comparing that
ratio with a corresponding one in regard to other materials.
For example, if ten chapters are devoted to events covering
one year, and one chapter is given to events covering one
hundred years, it is obvious when one compares the two
ratios of material to time that the author considers the
events which happened in the one year to be much more
important for his purposes than those which occurred in the
hundred-year span. The book of Genesis affords an excellent
illustration of the operation of such proportionate selectivity. Chapters 12-50, that is, thirty-nine chapters, are occupied with events which span a period of only four generations. On the other hand, the first eleven chapters cover a

period of many generations. It is apparent, then, that the author is calling particular attention to the Hebrew nation and especially to the patriarchs, and that what is contained in chapters 12-50 is more significant for the realization of his intent than the material found in chapters 1-11. This provides the observer with an insight which will be invaluable in the discovery of the writer's aim and message.

It should be noted, however, that the chronological element is not essential to the observation of proportion. In the logical type of literature, quantitative selectivity may simply involve devoting a greater amount of space to one idea or factor than to others. For instance, in John 17 about two-thirds of Jesus' prayer is given to indicating the bases for His petitions, whereas only one-third of the prayer is concerned with stating the actual petitions. This observation may well afford the grounds for using the law of proportion in the interpretation of John 17.[40]

(2) Non-quantitative Selectivity

Under this classification belong those events or ideas whose choice does not involve the principle of mass or quantity. The aforementioned event recorded in Genesis 12:10-20 may be cited as an example of this kind of selectivity. It is not one of many similar occurrences, at least in certain respects. In its context it stands as a singular event. It pictures a self-reliant Abraham, whereas the preceding and following events depict a man of faith. Now it is true that in Genesis 20 one finds almost an exact duplicate of this incident. However, in its immediate setting it is peculiar.

Regarding this type of event or idea, the observer should ask: "Why did the author include this particular event or idea? Why is it where it is? What does it contribute to the whole in view of its relations to the surrounding events or ideas?" If these and similar questions are answered, one will discover the relations and purpose implicit in this kind of selectivity.[41]

Exercise

Study the following passages from the standpoint of the principle of selectivity: Genesis 12-25, Judges, I and II Samuel, Acts, and I Corinthians. Look for quantitative and non-quantitative selectivity. Apply the principles and questions suggested in the preceding discussion.

7. **Miscellaneous Suggestions for Observing Structure** [42]

    a. Always look for relations. Remember that "things hook and eye together."

    b. Keep in mind the various laws of arrangement as you observe and use them in your structural analysis.

    c. Look for implicit relations as well as explicit ones.[43]

    d. Examine all connections closely, but especially conjunctions, prepositional phrases, and subordinate clauses. In the study of logical literature, such as is found in the Epistle to the Romans, pay particular attention to the connectives. Attempt to discover which are basic and which are secondary.[44] For examples see the "yet," "notwithstanding," and "therefore" in II Kings 17, and the "therefore" in Romans 1:24.

    e. The observer should be specific and exact in his analysis of structural relations. He should not be satisfied with a vague idea that for some undeterminable reason certain chapters are connected or belong together. Nor should he simply list the various connections of a passage.[45] Practice these suggestions in the observation of Leviticus and James I.

    f. Note carefully changes in pronouns and the implications of such changes for determining structure. (Mark 13, Jude)

g. Look for agreement between cause and effect, means and end, question and answer, need and remedy. (Matthew 18, Mark 13, Romans 1-11 and 12:1-15:13, Ephesians 1-3 and 4-6) [46]

h. Observe the tenses of verbs as well as their presence and predominance, and consider the significance of these factors for the discovery of literary arrangement. (Genesis 1:1-2:3, Exodus 6:1-8, Joshua 24:2-13, Hebrews 11:32-38)

i. In observing the structure of books, be on the alert for organizing expressions and for strategic centers which may be used as bases for surveying the whole. These may serve as "Empire State Buildings" from which one may view the outline and movement of a book. There are two primary types of strategic areas:

(1) *Historical*—This kind consists of events which are either pivotal or climactic. Joshua 6, 24:32-33, II Samuel 11, and I Kings 11 are illustrations of this type of strategic area. In this connection see the laws of cruciality and climax.

(2) *Literary*—This type consists of summary and interpretive passages. Genesis 45, Joshua 12, 23-24, Judges 2:11-23, II Kings 17, Acts 1:8, and Ephesians 4:1 afford examples of this kind of center. Note that some of these passages consist of events which, because of their very nature, are summarizations or interpretations. Genesis 45 and Joshua 23-24 belong in this category. In such passages the historical and literary types of strategic areas coincide.[47]

j. Compare and contrast the beginning and end of

books to find clues as to their content and arrangement. (Deuteronomy, Joshua)

k. In dealing with large bodies of material, first locate structural units or divisions. For example, Exodus has three main groups of chapters: first, 1-12:40, in Egypt; second, 12:41-18:27, to Sinai; and third, 19-40, at Sinai. Then, having found major divisions, attempt to discover the connections between these divisions. Do not be satisfied merely with finding main divisions, for structure involves more than the grouping of material. It is also concerned with the relations between the major groups of material. Therefore, having discovered the primary structural units, the observer ought to ask: "How are these main units related to each other? What function does each perform in regard to the others?" Practice these suggestions in the study of Genesis 25:19-36:43.

l. In observing narratives look for the development of the plot. (Genesis 3)

m. When examining epistles, look for epistolary structure. To discover what is involved in such structure, make a comparative study of the epistles.

n. When there is a promise, note its fulfilment; when the purpose is stated, look for its accomplishment.[48] (Joshua 1, John 20, I John 5, Jude)

o. Note refrains or repeated expressions which may indicate structure. (Genesis 1, Psalms, Matthew)

p. Observe negative and positive, general and specific approaches to the same problems or ideas. (Hebrews 3:7-4:16, 5:11-6:20, James 1, 2, 3, I Peter, I John 1)

q. Look for the use of parallelism, especially in poetic literature.[49] (Psalm 1)

r. Notice progression, how one thing leads to another. (John 17)

s. Look for changes in ideas and events. Attempt to discover when an author ceases discussing one thing and turns to another. (Romans 4)

t. Let the nature of the material being observed dictate its own structure. Be careful not to impose an arrangement on a passage.

u. Ask yourself these questions: "What is here? Why is it here? Why is it where it is? What difference would it make if it were omitted? What difference would it make if it were elsewhere?" [50]

v. Observe chief characters, events, and ideas, as well as indications of chronological and geographical movement or lack of movement. [51]

w. Use charts and outlines to indicate major structural relations. [52]

x. When discovering and analyzing structure, look for and use a single basis of composition. For example, if one section of a literary unit contains and is described by a geographical type of structure, another section of the same unit should not be described chronologically or historically. To be more concrete, if chapters 1-12 of Exodus are called "In Egypt," then chapters 19-40 should not be described as "The Law and the Tabernacle," but as the "At Sinai" division. The first two titles are not comparable; such a shifting of bases for indicating structure should be avoided unless, of course, the literature itself demands it.

y. Be aware of the distinction between historical and literary structure, as well as their relation to each other. For example, the connection between the Great Confession in Mark 8 and the Transfiguration in Mark 9 is primarily historical. When one wants to determine the relation between these two events, one first asks, "Why did the Transfiguration follow by six days the Great Confession? What is therefore the connection between them?" These questions involve historical structure, and it is through them that the reader of Mark arrives at the reasons for the author's selection and inclusion of the two aforementioned events, that is, their literary relations. Thus in this instance historical and literary structure are essentially identical. However, there are occasions when, although the literary arrangement follows in general the historical or chronological order, because of selectivity the author's use of literary composition transcends that which is inherent in historical structure. For example, a writer may select two events, the first of which precedes the second from the standpoint of chronology. However, these events may have no specific historical connections. By placing them side by side in terms of literary structure, thereby utilizing one or more of the laws of arrangement, the author may convey a message which is completely distinct from what is inherent in the historical sequence of the events. Genesis 38 and 39 may afford an illustration of this. Furthermore, there are instances when Biblical writers rearrange the events so that they no longer follow their historical or chronological order. In such cases also literary structure is distinct from historical structure. When one observes this latter phenomenon, one should pay close attention to the literary arrangement and inquire as to the reasons for the alteration of the historical sequence. Luke 8 provides an example of a passage where the chrono-

logical order is set aside. Compare Luke 8 with
Mark 3 to see wherein this is true.

Exercise

Keeping in mind the structural relations and the materials
for effecting them discussed in the preceding pages, observe
the structure of the following units: Genesis 1:1-2:3, I and
II Chronicles, Nehemiah, Job, Malachi, Galatians, Philemon, Hebrews 1:4-4:13, and I Peter 1:3-2:10. Attempt to
keep before you the other principles and suggestions given.

C. Observation of General Literary Forms

The third constituent of a passage which one needs to
observe is its general literary form. This element is distinct
from both those of terms and structure, for the same terms
and the same structural relations effected by the same materials may be utilized to compose different kinds of literature.
Therefore, to note terms and structural connections is not
sufficient for thorough observation; one must also see the
general type of literature used by an author.

The primary types of literary forms will now be described
briefly and illustrated. An attempt will also be made to indicate some of the factors which make them significant for
interpretation in order to stimulate the observer to note
them carefully. In reading this material it should be remembered that various kinds of literature are sometimes used in
combinations, and further that there are different ways of
classifying literary forms. The following discussion suggests
one means of classification.

1. Discoursive and Logical Literature

In this category belong all reports of extended discourses
and all those writings which involve a presentation of ideas
in argumentative form. Epistolary literature, some of the

prophetic sermons, and the longer discourses of Jesus may be placed in this classification.

This type of literature appeals primarily to the intellect. Therefore, the importance of recognizing it is that an awareness of its presence will lead to a careful observation of its logical development; and it is only when special attention is given to its rational method that valid interpretation will result.

2. Prose Narrative

This sort of literary form is the chief kind employed, for example, in the book of Genesis and in the Gospels. Its primary purpose is not to relate impersonal historical facts, but rather to present evangelical or theological history. It therefore contains personalized history in the form of stories and biographical sketches. Its appeal is primarily to the imagination and to the emotions. Therefore, to attempt to interpret it without the liberal use of the imagination in its legitimate sense is to guarantee either partial or faulty interpretation.

It should also be remembered that prose narrative often contains some details which are not too significant for exposition, but rather have as their main purpose the completion of the color of the story. When one observes the presence of the prose narrative type of form, therefore, one should be careful not to press unduly every detail. One should make a distinction between that which is essential and that which is ornamental.

3. Poetry

Scriptural poetry has three main characteristics. First, it frequently utilizes figurative language. Second, it is emotional in nature. Someone has said that "poetry is the emotion of life made audible." And third, it employs parallelisms of different types, such as those which are synonymous, antithetic, and synthetic.[58] Therefore, to be aware of the presence of the poetic form is to be on guard against its misinterpretation. For when one remembers that the poet employs flexible language, and that he expresses feelings rather than rigid logical concepts, one will not attempt to expound his language as if he utilized a literal, scientific vocabulary, or examine his statements at every turn for a precise, systematic theology. The awareness of the use of parallelisms will also be of great help in assuring correct exposition.

4. Drama and Dramatic Prose

The dramatic method involves primarily the personification, particularization, and vivid description of events or ideas for the sake of their moving effect. It is undoubtedly closely related to the poetic expression of truth. In view of these facts, one must determine whether a writer is speaking in terms of actual history or whether he is using the dramatic approach to make more striking the truth he is conveying. For example, one should realize that in chapter 2 of his book the prophet Isaiah may be utilizing drama in his description of the future place and destiny of Jerusalem, and that it would not be safe to assume that what the prophet declares there is intended to be literally factual. Of course, one must beware of classifying all or most of the literature of the Old Testament in the category of drama. One should study the literature itself to ascertain its own claim as to its literary form, and one should avoid superimposing the dramatic approach on actual history. At the same time, the observer must recognize that the dramatic method is a legitimate form of literary communication, and that its presence needs to be taken into account in the process of interpretation.

5. Parabolic Literature

The parabolic form employs the principle of analogy. This is indicated by the signification of the word "parable," which is a combination of the Greek terms *para* and *ballo* and therefore literally connotes "that which is thrown or put forth beside something else." Thus a parable consists of two parts, the spiritual truth which is being illustrated, and the brief physical narrative which is placed beside it for the purpose of clarification. Excellent examples of parabolic literature may be found in Matthew 13, Mark 4, and Luke 15.

6. Apocalyptic Literature

The term "apocalypse" literally means "uncovering" or "revelation." Apocalyptic literature is often characterized by the use of symbolism and descriptions of visions which are predictive in nature. The book of Daniel in the Old Testament and the book of the Revelation in the New Testament are good illustrations of these characteristics of apocalyptic literature.[54]

D. Observation of Atmosphere

The fourth element in the observing process is that of atmosphere. By atmosphere is meant the underlying tone or spirit of a passage, which though intangible, is nevertheless real. Some of the moods by which a portion may be characterized are those of despair, thanksgiving, awe, urgency, joy, humility, or tenderness.

At times the mood of a passage cannot be determined until the reader has engaged seriously in the process of interpretation. On the other hand, it is often true that thorough observation will reveal its underlying atmosphere. In any case, until one has discovered the mood of a portion of Scripture, one has not come into vital contact with its author's mind and spirit.

It should be noted that some passages may involve a combination of various moods. In fact, there may be a drastic change of atmosphere within one unit of Scripture. Therefore, one should be careful to observe all of the atmospheric elements of a passage.

IV. AIDS TO OBSERVATION IN GENERAL

A. Use a pencil or pen while observing. Writing down one's observations is beneficial for several reasons, not the least of which is the fact that it impresses them upon one's mind. Writing is a great aid to memory.

B. There are two primary approaches in the observation of a passage. One type of observation begins with a detailed noting of particulars and proceeds to the observation of the whole. The second kind of observation begins with a survey of the whole, progresses to the noting of particulars, and moves finally to a synthesis of the particulars. Both of these types are valid and useful. The first reflects the usual process followed in the reading of a passage, for it involves beginning from the beginning and moving term by term, phrase by phrase, and clause by clause to the conclusion. The writer has found that this procedure is more helpful in the observation of a relatively short passage, where perspective is not so important. The second kind of observation is most salutary when one is dealing with a longer body of material, where perspective is essential to effective observation. However, the reader is urged to experiment with both types and to determine for himself which best suits him.

C. This calls attention to the fact that two errors should be avoided in observation: first, seeing the whole without noting details; and second, seeing details and missing the whole. *Observation should be both analytical and synthetical.* In fact, analytical observation should have as its objective synthetical observation. It is for this reason that the observational process should always culminate with a view of the whole.

D. A further distinction should be made between the course followed in the observation of a paragraph or

segment and that followed in the observation of a
subsection, section, division, or book.[55] Obviously the
examination of the second or longer type of passage
cannot be as minute as the examination of the first,
at least in one's initial approach. Therefore, in observing a larger body of material, it is well to scan it
several times if possible, noting *key* terms, phrases, or
statements; *chief* persons, places, and events; structural units; *major* relations; and *crucial* chapters.
The observer can then concentrate on those elements
and sections which seem to be most significant.

In order to get the contents and relations of a
longer passage before one, it is often helpful to name
the chapters as one scans them. This is especially true
in the study of narrative portions.[56]

By all means, one should not become entangled in
minutia when making an initial approach to a long
passage.

E.   In recording detailed observations, enumerate them
so as to make them distinct from each other. Use
some means, such as underlining or encircling, to indicate major observations. Utilize charts to show
main observations, especially in the realm of structural relations.[57] Find ways of organizing your observations so that they will be accessible with the least
possible effort. Give specific chapter and verse references for each observation so that there will be no
question as to the particulars of the text upon which
the observations are based.

F.   Although observation should result in seeing every
particular of a passage, when recording observations
one should write down only that which is noteworthy.
One should not list as observations, for example,
every "the" which appears in a passage. Only in those
cases when the term "the" is significant should it be
recorded. Mark 15:39 is an example of such an in-

stance.[58] Unless this type of discretion is applied, the process of listing observations will become inefficient and discouraging.[59]

G. When recording observations, avoid simply copying the words of the text. Indicate something about them. For example, when observing Isaiah 55, one might note these facts:

> The passage begins with "Ho." (v. 1)
> The passage is addressed to "everyone that thirsteth." (v. 1)

Such a procedure will promote awareness and help to fix in mind the observations made.

H. The four elements of a passage, namely, terms, structure, literary form, and atmosphere, need not and should not be noted separately. For instance, the observer should not look first for all the terms of a passage before he notes its structural relations. Now it is true that there is a certain order inherent in the observation of the components of a passage. One cannot note a connection between two terms before one observes the presence of each of the terms. Furthermore, both literary form and atmosphere cannot be observed with finality in some instances until the whole unit has been examined, since they sometimes change within it. However, it still remains that all of the elements of a passage need not and should not be observed in a rigid order. A person may well note the use of two terms and then note the relation between them. He may then proceed to the observation of more terms, together with the relations and interrelations between them. Thus a list of observations will involve an intermingling of term-al, structural, formal, and atmospheric observations.[60]

I. Observe every passage as if you had never seen it before. Let every approach be a fresh one. Refer to

previous observations only after you have completed
your latest observational approach. It is said that Toscanini never looks at a score of music without seeing
it as though he had never seen it and was seeing it for
the first time.[61]

J. Discipline yourself to see how many different observations you can make on a given passage. Learn to
spend hours in the process of observation. It is the
disciplined observer who is the effective and thorough
observer.[62]

K. The principle set forth by the following statement is
an excellent aid to observation: "An observer will
have his eyes open to notice anything which according to received theories ought not to happen, for
these are the facts which serve as clues to new discoveries." Joseph's gracious attitude toward his scheming
brothers is an illustration of this. (Genesis 37-50) In
fact, it is frequently helpful to contrast what is found
in a passage to that which might be found there but
is not. For example, the Psalmist says, "The Lord is
my shepherd, *I* shall not want." He does not say,
"The Lord is *a* shepherd, *I* shall not want."

L. Asking oneself the questions implied in the following
lines is often helpful:

I have six faithful serving men
Who taught me all I know.
Their names are *What* and *Where* and *When*
And *How* and *Why* and *Who*.[63]

M. Note any significant omissions as well as the events
and ideas which are included. Stevenson once re-
marked: "To omit . . . is the one art of literature:
'If I knew how to omit, I should ask no other knowledge.' "[64] If this statement even approximates the
truth, as it undoubtedly does, then it is of supreme
importance that the observer note carefully an au-

thor's omissions if he is to discover the author's
mind.[65]

N. Compare and contrast observations. Dr. Alexander
Graham Bell's formula for a liberal self-education
was: Observe! Remember! Compare! [66]

O. It is often useful to compare and contrast various passages or books, such as the books of the Kings with I
and II Chronicles, the minor prophets with each
other, parallel Gospel accounts, and the Synoptics
with the Fourth Gospel.

P. Compare and contrast the different translations of the
Scriptures.

Q. At times try thinking in terms of writing a newspaper
report or painting a picture of a passage. These and
similar means cause one to observe more exactly. Try
this suggestion in the study of Exodus 35-40.

R. Make rough maps indicating the geography of a unit.
This is especially helpful in the observation of such
books as Genesis, Exodus, Joshua, the Gospels, and
the Acts.

S. In observing biographical material, note the characteristics of the men involved, their concept of and
attitude toward God, their actions, reactions, and motives.

T. In examining epistolary literature, note the following factors: the identity and characteristics of the
writers; the location, characteristics, and problems of
the recipients; the answers given to their problems;
the occasion and purpose of the letter; its literary features, leading ideas, and central truth.

U. Note marginal readings. Someone has said that "the
wisdom of the revisers is in the margin."

V. Look for the concepts of God, Christ, man, sin, and
redemption, since these represent the primary themes
with which Biblical authors are concerned.

W. In dealing with segments in the narrative type of literature, such as the Gospels, it is usually helpful to name the paragraphs. Such a procedure aids one in noting and remembering the main characters and events and enables one to observe, record, and recall relations.

There are two primary types of paragraph titles: first, the *descriptive* title, which delineates the subject matter in terms of place, people, or event; and second, the *analytical* or *interpretive* title, which is based on an exposition of the material. A descriptive title for Mark 7:24-30 might be "The Syrophoenician Woman." An analytical title for the same paragraph might be "The Universality of Faith." It is obvious that the kind of paragraph title in which the observer ought primarily to be interested is the descriptive title, since the analytical title is more interpretive in nature.

A paragraph title should have the following *characteristics: brevity*—two or three words if possible; *memorableness*—imaginative, catching; *uniqueness*—applicable only to óne paragraph; *suggestiveness*—recalls the content of the paragraph; *suitableness*—befitting the paragraph; and *individuality*—helpful to the particular individual using it. Sometimes it is possible so to name paragraphs as to suggest the relations between them.

The naming of paragraphs should never become a cursory practice. One should be conscious of the reasons for it and should engage in it only when so doing enhances one's study.

X. Be able to distinguish between an observation, an interpretation, and an application. Avoid application altogether in the observing process and keep interpretation to a minimum. The latter suggestion does not apply to the bridge between observation and interpretation, namely, the interpretive question, which will be discussed later.[67] Further, it should be remembered that some interpretation must enter into the observational process. For there is no clear-cut line of demarcation between the first two steps of inductive study and it is infeasible to manufacture one. For example, the observer marks the use of the term "but" in a certain statement. If he were to limit himself strictly to observation, he could not even call attention to the fact that "but" involves contrast; for such a notation is the beginning of the process of interpretation, which is further completed by answering the question, "What is the meaning of the structural relation of contrast as it is used in this instance?" However, to restrain one from indicating that "but" reveals contrast would be to doom observation to an impractical and insignificant role. For these reasons the notation that "but" involves contrast should be included in the first step of methodical study, as has been suggested in the preceding pages.[68] This may be done because the interpretation involved in such an observation is so self-evident that there is no danger of arriving at conclusions without first examining all the evidence. However, when it comes to the more intricate interpretations, one ought to await the general completion of the observational process. Thus although interpretation cannot be fully eliminated from observation, it should certainly be kept at a safe minimum.

To put it another way, neither too little nor too much should be expected from observation. The process of observation should eventuate in some significant discoveries, although it is true that all one's findings will not be equally significant. On the other hand, observation should not be construed so as to include the whole study process. Such a view would reduce Scriptural study to one step and would tend to

remove both inductiveness and methodicalness from
it. One should rather understand the limited though
important purpose of observation and do that which
will result in its accomplishment. This purpose is to
become aware of the terms, structure, literary form,
and atmosphere of a passage. The meaning and application of that of which the observer becomes aware
should generally await the further phases of study.[69]

V. SUMMARY OF OBSERVATION

There are two marks which characterize the efficient observer: *awareness* and *thoroughness*. He is not mechanical
in his observation. Rather he is alive to the contents of a
passage. He perceives, he actually sees. And he sees all the
components of a passage. He takes nothing for granted. He
disciplines himself to absorb consciously the entire unit. He
marks attentively *each term,* because he knows that any artist
who is worthy of the name makes a thoughtful and purposeful selection of terminology. He also notes carefully the *relations and interrelations between terms.* He keeps his eyes
open to the smallest as well as the largest connections. He
pays close attention to the *general literary form* and *atmosphere* of a passage. In brief, all the constituents of a Biblical
unit become a part of the consciousness of the proficient
observer.[70]

VI. EXERCISE ON OBSERVATION

A. Note carefully the terms, structural relations, general
literary forms, and atmospheres of the following segments: Leviticus 16, Psalms 19, 24, 44, 51, 150, Isaiah
1:2-31, Matthew 11, 18, John 9-10, 15, Romans 8.

B. Observe also the *key* terms, *main* relations, general
literary forms, and underlying tones of the following
books: Ruth, Ezra, Esther, Ezekiel, Hosea, Joel,

Jonah, Zephaniah, Haggai, Colossians, I and II Peter, and the Revelation.

General Directions—Record all noteworthy observations. Attempt to classify them as to whether they are term-al (T), structural (S), form-al (F), or atmospheric (A). Remember to keep interpretation to a minimum and to avoid all application. Apply the principles and suggestions of the preceding material.

NOTES

1. *Webster's Collegiate Dictionary,* Fifth Edition.
2. Kuist, H. T., *These Words Upon Thy Heart,* p. 79. For a more complete discussion of some of the terms used in this manual, see the following references: Eberhardt, C. R., *The Bible in the Making of Ministers,* pp. 115-157; and Kuist, H. T., *These Words Upon Thy Heart,* pp. 45-62, 67-70, 99-100, 101-102.
3. Coulton, G. G., *Five Centuries of Religion,* Volume I, p. xxxvii.
4. Jowett, J. H., *Brooks by the Traveller's Way,* pp. 78-79.
5. MacFarlan, R., excerpt from *Our Human Comedy* in *Coronet,* July, 1946.
6. In this connection see *The Student, the Fish, and Agassiz,* which the writer would like to quote in full if it were not for the shortage of space. It may be found in C. R. Eberhardt's *The Bible in the Making of Ministers,* pp. 134-138.
7. The forthcoming analysis must necessarily be concerned with the grammatical concepts and terminology of English, Hebrew, and Greek, since methodical Bible study is concerned ultimately with literature in all three of these languages. This fact raises several problems which will be discussed briefly at this point.

One of these is the fact that in order to understand fully the following material, the reader needs to be acquainted with English, Hebrew, and Greek grammar. It would therefore be ideal if at this stage of the discussion complete treatments of the grammar of these languages could be incorporated. For obvious reasons this cannot be done. Reference will therefore be made to some outstanding grammatical discussions of the languages in question with the hope that the reader will utilize them to become better acquainted with the necessary grammatical tools to be used in methodical Bible study.

However, even the inclusion of these references will not solve the grammatical problem for all those who use this book. For some will not have sufficient knowledge to benefit by them, since they will not know Hebrew and Greek. Of course, it would be salutary for such to learn these languages; for a knowledge of them is essential for *thoroughgoing* study. However, short of this, one can be confident that the vernacular will convey most of the grammatical factors necessary for understanding Biblical writings. If this were not true, the bulk of Christendom would be unqualified for Bible study, and the Bible would be accessible only to a privileged few.

Another problem which the forthcoming presentation must face is connected with its attempt to synthesize the major grammatical features of three distinct and different languages. Such a synthesis will undoubtedly have its shortcomings. But these shortcomings are the same ones faced in translating one language into another, and yet this does not deter us from translating, because translations are necessary. Likewise, though the synthesis entailed in the forthcoming discussion will have its recognized limitations, it will be done because it is essential for the development of a methodical approach to Biblical units.

8. The occurrence of non-routine terms increases in the more logical type of literature, such as the Pauline Epistles.

9. This distinction between the literal and the figurative holds also in larger units of expression, such as phrases, clauses, sentences, paragraphs, etc.

10. In this regard note the terms of Mark 9:42-50. A newspaper account once appeared of a man who interpreted the term "cut" literally instead of figuratively and consequently went to the woodshed and amputated his arm.

11. Other identifying expressions are sometimes used, such as "gerund" and "participle." Pronouns may be identified further in terms of the following categories: personal, relative, demonstrative, intensive, reflexive, reciprocal, interrogative, and indefinite.

12. For a fuller discussion of these kinds of speech and their inflections, see the indexes of: Kierzek, John, *The Macmillan Handbook of English;* Dana and Mantey, *A Manual Grammar of the Greek New Testament;* and Gesenius, *Hebrew Grammar.* For a more complete discussion of terms, see M. J. Adler's *How To Read a Book,* pp. 185-208.

13. The reader will need to examine the context to discover whether "structure" is being used broadly or in a limited sense. It should further be noted that "structure" will be used synonymously with "composition," although "composition" may connote means more than end. For Ruskin defines "composition" as the ". . . putting of several things together, so as to make *one* thing out of them." (Appendix of H. T. Kuist's *These Words Upon Thy Heart,* p. 161, J. Ruskin's "Essay on Composition.") "Structure," on the other hand, primarily denotes to this writer's mind the end product, that is, the framework which is formed by the arrangement of the different parts. However, in the last analysis both "composition" and "structure" must involve both means and end, since these two factors are ultimately inseparable.

14. For more complete definitions of these terms consult your dictionary. Note that although a necessary distinction is made between "clause" and "sentence," they are sometimes identical, since some sentences consist of single clauses.

15. The use of "subsection" is unnecessary in the structural analysis of certain books. This may also be true in regard to some of the other structural units.

16. Taylor, H. O., *The Mediaeval Mind,* Volume I, p. 20.

17. Ante, p. 5.

18. Ante, p. 20.

19. To substantiate these statements one need only examine some of the world's great paintings, musical compositions, and literary works.

20. The term "paragraph" is used in the ideal sense in these statements. It does not necessarily refer to particular paragraphs in a particular translation, but to groups of sentences which actually form units of thought and expression.

21. *Webster's Collegiate Dictionary*, Fifth Edition. See also Dana and Mantey, *A Manual Grammar of the Greek New Testament*, pp. 59ff.

22. These clauses may involve the various moods, such as indicative, subjunctive, imperative, etc.

23. Most of these descriptive terms are borrowed from Dana and Mantey, *A Manual Grammar of the Greek New Testament*, pp. 268-303.

24. The Revised Standard Version will be used for all New Testament references and the American Revised Version for Old Testament references.

25. Other ways of expressing temporal and local connections may be noted by scanning the historical books of the Old Testament, the Gospels, or the book of the Acts.

26. Comparison, contrast, enumeration, or progression from the general to the specific may be involved in this type of relation.

27. In this connection see the following: Kierzek, John, *The Macmillan Handbook of English*, index; Dana and Mantey, *A Manual Grammar of the Greek New Testament*, pp. 239-267; and Gesenius, *Hebrew Grammar*, index.

28. This suggestion brings to mind the fact that the element of position often plays an important role in the syntax of a sentence. In both Hebrew and Greek the relative position of a term in the word order of a sentence may indicate its importance or the terms with which it should be most closely associated. For examples see Genesis 1:1, Exodus 21:3, Matthew 5:17, John 1:1, and I Corinthians 5:3-5. At times the English translation is unable to convey fully this positional factor.

29. For another example of grammatical analysis, see L. M. Sweet's *The Study of the English Bible*, Appendix C. Incidentally, diagramming is an excellent means of coming to grips with the relations within clauses and sentences. If the reader is not acquainted with the techniques of diagram-

ming, let him refer to Kierzek, John, *The Macmillan Handbook of English*, pp. 31-49.

30. The important chronological connection suggested by the prepositional phrase "after six days" is a relation between paragraphs and segments rather than between two sentences within the same paragraph. It is for this reason that it is not given due consideration at this place.

31. Ante, pp. 31-32.

32. Ante, p. 20.

33. To this writer's mind one of the weaknesses of the traditional approach to exegesis has been its emphasis on grammatical relations at the expense of a sensitivity to literary structure.

34. There may be some question as to whether the law of continuation should be included in this list. It may be maintained that such a law is merely a general description of progression or elaboration, which may in turn involve climax, continuity, etc. However, it will be retained in order to insure completeness, because in certain cases one may raise a legitimate question as to whether any of the other structural relations are present.

35. For a fuller discussion of some of these laws, see H. T. Kuist's *These Words Upon Thy Heart*, pp. 80-87, and the Appendix of the same book, which contains John Ruskin's "Essay on Composition." Note that the writer of this manual has redefined and adapted some of the laws described in these references. Note also that the laws of principality and radiation, which are listed by Ruskin, are not included here. The reason is that to this writer's mind these laws involve ends rather than means and are therefore different from the other structural relations. For example, the superior high priesthood of Jesus is made *principal* in Hebrews by *means* of repetition and continuity.

36. See Romans 6 as an example.

37. These statements may be applied to other phases of methodical study. Also, it should not be inferred from them that the inductive approach does not result in strong convictions. However, these facts should be noted with regard to inductive convictions: first, they are based on concrete data

and not on authoritarian grounds; second, they are communicated to others on the same grounds on which they are derived, not by authority but by an examination of particulars; and third, in any case they are *never forced* upon an individual.

In connection with this last point, the writer has followed the practice of expressing his own convictions in those cases where the evidence appears to him to be conclusive. But after so doing, he makes it clear to the members of the class that they must make up their own minds. One finds that such an approach is pedagogically sound; for the students are much more receptive than they would be to an authoritarian approach and their decisions tend to be inductive rather than deductive.

38. See the Appendix for more complete examples of the observation of literary structure.

39. The principle of purposive selectivity applies to terms and general literary forms as well as structure.

40. At times the problem of the accessibility of materials may arise in the application of the law of proportion; for there is the possibility that only certain materials were available and that this fact limited the author's choice. In such cases all the obtainable data must be studied in order to arrive at a valid conclusion. In so doing one should remember that an author is not obligated to include all of the subject matter which is accessible, even if it be limited in scope.

41. Although in this discussion the selectivity of events and ideas has been stressed for the sake of expediency, it should not be inferred that the law of selectivity is operative only in historical and logical types of literature. Selectivity is inherent in all literature and, in fact, in all art. The observation of selectivity is therefore also helpful in the examination of biographical, geographical, and chronological types of arrangement.

42. The purpose of this and comparable lists is twofold: first, to stress and apply some important points which have been mentioned already; and second, to indicate some significant principles and practices not noted in the preceding discussion.

43. Ante, pp. 38-39.
44. Ante, p. 39.
45. Ante, pp. 53-54.
46. Ante, p. 52. The law of harmony is basically involved in this suggestion.
47. This distinction is meant to emphasize the fact that some areas are strategic primarily because of their place in the movement of history, whereas others are important primarily from the standpoint of literary structure. In this connection note the discussion of historical and literary structure on pp. 66-67.
48. Ante, p. 52.
49. Post, pp. 69-70.
50. Ante, pp. 59-62.
51. Ante, pp. 55-59.
52. See the Appendix for examples of structural charts.
53. Consult M. S. Terry's *Biblical Hermeneutics*, pp. 144-156.
54. Note that the more minor literary forms, such as proverbs, fables, riddles, allegories, typologies, and symbolisms were not included in this list. For a helpful discussion of literary forms, see "The Bible as Literature," by L. B. Longacre, in *The Abingdon Bible Commentary*, pp. 19-25. Further consideration of some of the literary forms together with bibliographical suggestions will be found in the later pages of this manual. (Post, pp. 148-150.)
55. This distinction is applicable only in relation to long books. It does not hold true in the study of brief books, such as Philemon.
56. For hints concerning the naming of chapters, see the discussion on the naming of paragraphs, p. 77.
57. Examples of these may be found in the Appendix.
58. In this case the American Revised Version was used. Note the marginal reference.
59. Ante, pp. 34-35.
60. The terms "term-al" and "form-al" have been coined for the sake of expediency. In the first instance "terminological" could be used, but it is rather cumbersome. In the second case one could utilize "formal" except for the fact that it usually has different connotations from those desired here.

The writer is indebted to the Rev. Elmer Parsons for suggesting these terms.

61. Gilman, L., *Toscanini and Great Music*, p. 2.

62. Ante, p. 33.

63. Kipling, R.

64. James, W., *The Varieties of Religious Experience*, pp. 290-291.

65. Ante, pp. 59-62.

66. See Reprint from *The Reader's Digest*, February 1922, entitled "How to Keep Young Mentally."

67. Post, pp. 97ff.

68. Ante, p. 42.

69. Ante, pp. 31-32. The full use of this list of suggestions would involve interpretation as well as observation. Therefore, only those phases should be followed at this stage which are observational in nature. The remaining ones should be kept in mind as guides in the interpretive process.

70. The author regrets that space does not permit detailed examples at this point of the various phases of observation. However, the reader will find a list of observations on Psalm 23 in the section on interpretation. He will also find examples of structural observation in the Appendix. It is hoped that these will suffice.

CHAPTER TWO

Interpretation

CHAPTER TWO

Interpretation

ONCE THE COMPONENTS of a passage have been noted, which is the first step of induction, the next logical step is to determine their meaning. Thus the second phase of methodical study is interpretation.

I. PURPOSE OF INTERPRETATION AND FUNCTION OF THE INTERPRETER

In his first volume of *Five Centuries of Religion,* Coulton makes this statement: "The historian must strive by the closest insight to identify himself with the past . . ." [1] In his book *Toscanini and Great Music,* Gilman repeatedly uses the term "re-creation" to describe the purpose of musical interpretation and the function of Toscanini as interpreter. [2] Thus both Coulton and Gilman suggest the same principle, namely, that *the problem of interpretation is the problem of re-creation.* This principle applies not only to history and music, but to everything else which requires explanation.

Webster defines "re-creation" as "reanimation, the giving fresh life to something." [3] To re-create the Scriptures, then, is to expound them in such a way as to cause the written word to become the living word. This can be accomplished only through *empathy,* that is, "the imaginative projection of one's own consciousness into another being." [4] Thus the process of re-creation involves such a complete identification of the interpreter with the authors of the Bible that he re-lives the experiences which were entailed in its writing. It means recapturing the attitudes, motives, thoughts, and emotions of its writers and of those concerning whom they wrote.

Since the re-creation of Biblical literature is accomplished primarily through empathy, the use of the imagination becomes essential. Most of us are afraid to utilize our imagination because we inevitably relate it to that which is fantastic, fictional, and subjective. Now it is true that the imagination may be used in such a way so as to be characterized by these qualities. On the other hand, it may also be sanctified so that it may perform a legitimate and indispensable function in Scriptural exposition. For the imagination may supply the magic carpet which transports us to Biblical times and enables us to live and think and feel with the writers and characters of the Scriptures. It may enable us, for example, to experience the thoughts and emotions of Abraham when he was asked by God to sacrifice Isaac, the son of promise. (Genesis 22) It may provide the means by which to audioize and visualize the events which occurred in the giving of the law at Mt. Sinai. (Exodus 19-20) It may supply the instrument through which one may relive the experiences of Jesus Himself, so that one may discover the mind which was in Christ Jesus.

The following story was once told of Toscanini.

While rehearsing Beethoven's 'Ninth Symphony', the musicians responded with a particular sensitivity to Toscanini's every wish and desire. What resulted was a performance that moved the men of the orchestra to a spontaneous ovation. They rose to their feet and cheered the little man who had just given them such a new and wonderful insight into the music. Desperately, Toscanini tried to stop them, waving his arms wildly, shouting to them. Finally when the ovation subsided, he said in a broken voice: 'It isn't me men—it's Beethoven.' [5]

Such re-creation should be the goal of the interpreter of the Scriptures as well. And when it occurs, men will similarly recognize its worth and know for certain that the Bible has come alive.

II. MAJOR PHASES OF INTERPRETATION

One of the dangers in relation to interpretation is that it can be incomplete, for there is much more to it than immediately meets the eye. It involves not only the matter of definition, to which some limit interpretation, but other phases as well. In order to help avoid this danger of superficiality, attention will be called at the outset to the main facets of thorough interpretation. It should be noted that they overlap to some degree.

A. Definitive Phase

The first aspect of interpretation is that of discovering the basic meaning of the particulars of a passage. In a sense it corresponds to the function of dictionaries and lexicons.

This is especially true in relation to terms. For example, the term "love" found in Deuteronomy 6:5 may be defined as follows: to have a deep affection for, to long for, to desire. However, essentially the same explanatory procedure should be applied to other components of a passage, such as its structural relations. One should discover, for instance, what is meant by the biographical contrast between Solomon and David suggested in I Kings 11:4. That is, one should attempt to explain wherein the two men were actually different. In so doing one defines the relation of contrast as it is used in this particular instance.

B.   Rational Phase [6]

Having discovered the basic meaning of the components of a passage, it is then necessary to attempt to find the reasons which underlie them. Such an attempt is concerned with two factors: first, the *general reasons* why Biblical statements are made—wherein they are true and necessary; and second, the *immediate reasons or purposes* for their expression—their relevance to their literary context and specific historical situation. Both of these are not pertinent in the case of every Biblical component, and at times they are undiscoverable. But an awareness of them and their use whenever possible is supremely important for incisive interpretation.

To illustrate, one should attempt to discern these facts regarding the use of "love" in Deuteronomy 6:5: first, the *reasons* for the truth and necessity of the statement that the Israelites should love Jehovah, that is, the reasons why this exhortation is valid; and second, the *purposes* for the exhortation to love Jehovah in the concrete setting in which it was made.

C.   Implicational Phase

A statement always implicates more than it says explicitly, for it is the outgrowth of certain presuppositions and in turn becomes the presupposition for other ideas. The interrelatedness of facts makes this inevitable. Facts are so intertwined that a person cannot accept one without accepting many others with it. Thus if one would understand fully the significance of Deuteronomy 6:5, one needs to search for the widespread implications of the exhortation to love Jehovah.[7]

III.   SPECIFIC PROCESS OF INTERPRETATION

Three basic steps are needed to realize the purpose and to effect the various phases of interpretation: first, interpretive questions; second, interpretive answers; and third, interpretive integration and summarization. Each of these will now be discussed.

A. Interpretive Questions

1. Meaning, Function, and Importance of Interpretive Questions

Interpretive questions are those questions arising from and based on the observations of terms, structure, general literary forms, and atmosphere whose answers will result in the discovery of their full meaning. In fact, they frame in question form the various phases of interpretation, namely, definition, reasons, and implications.[8]

The interpretive question is in reality the intermediate step between observation and interpretation. At times, therefore, it is actually a part of observation; at other times it arises after observation is virtually complete. In any case it is the essential bridge between observation and interpretation, and without it observation may become a shallow and almost worthless practice.

To illustrate how the use of the interpretive question results in the discovery of the meaning of one's observations, the partial text of an advertisement for Mortimer J. Adler's *How To Read a Book* will be inserted at this point. The advertisement appeared in the *New York Times* on April 10, 1940, under the picture of a puzzled adolescent reading his first love letter.

How To Read a Love Letter

This young man has just received his first love letter. He may have read it three or four times, but he is just beginning. To read it as accurately as he would like, would require several dictionaries and a good deal of close work with a few experts of etymology and philology.

However, he will do all right without them.

He will ponder over the exact shade of meaning of every word, every comma. She has headed the letter 'Dear John'. What, he asks himself, is the exact significance of those words? Did she refrain from saying 'Dearest' because she was bashful? Would 'My Dear' have sounded too formal?

Jeepers, maybe she would have said 'Dear So-and-So' to anybody!

A worried frown will now appear on his face. But it disappears as soon as he really gets to thinking about the first sentence. She certainly wouldn't have written *that* to anybody!

And so he works his way through the letter, one moment perched blissfully on a cloud, the next moment huddled miserably behind an eight-ball. It has started a hundred questions in his mind. He could quote it by heart. In fact, he will—to himself—for weeks to come.

The advertisement continues: "If people read books with anything like the same concentration, we'd be a race of mental giants."

The reader will note the outstanding place occupied in this advertisement by interpretive questions. They grow out of the observation of the contents of the letter and they form the link between them and their exposition. The interpretive question in connection with Scriptural study will perform the same function.

In view of the purpose of interpretive questions, their importance cannot be overemphasized. As significant as observation is, its value will not be realized apart from the use of interpretive questions or their equivalent. A certain student, realizing this fact, said to his teacher: "If I only had you to sit next to me while I study in order to ask questions, then I would be able to grasp the meaning of these passages." [9]

2. Types of Interpretive Questions

The various kinds of interpretive questions may be classified in terms of two categories: the components of the passage with which they are concerned, and the phases of interpretation which they express.

In regard to the first category, interpretive questions may be classified as term-al, structural, form-al, or atmospheric, depending on the component which they involve.

In relation to the second category, there are several classes of interpretive questions. The three *primary* ones correspond to the major phases of interpretation previously discussed: first, the definitive or explanatory question—what does this mean? second, the rational question—why is this said and why is it said here? and third, the implicational question—what does this imply? Then there are four *subordinate* questions: first, the identifying question—who or what is involved? second, the modal question—how is this accomplished? third, the temporal question—when is this accomplished? and fourth, the local question—where is this accomplished?

The following facts should be noted regarding these questions.

First, the two categories will be combined in the identification of particular questions. For example, an interpretive question which purposes to define a term will be called "definitive term-al," whereas one which attempts to ascertain the reasons for a structural relation will be called "rational structural."

Second, at times some of these questions may be observational in nature, depending on the character of the passage. For example, the temporal question may be answered by the simple process of noting the terms of a passage. At other times the answer may require extensive exposition. Note also that one question which might be expected was not included, namely, "What is here?" The reason is that this question is primarily observational in nature and is asked as part of the observational step. As a matter of fact, the whole process of observation is an answer to this question. However, one discovers that the observational question will sometimes reassert itself during interpretation, especially in connection with structure. For, as was already stressed, certain structural observations cannot be made until there has occurred at least a partial completion of the interpretive step.[10]

Third, not all of these questions are relevant to every particular in every passage.

Fourth, these questions are general in nature and should be adapted in view of the particular portion being studied.

Fifth, the lines of demarcation between these questions are by no means clear-cut, for they are often progressive in nature, each successive question being an extension of the preceding one.

3. Illustrations of Types of Interpretive Questions [11]

a. *Individual Illustrations of Interpretive Questions*

For the most part the following illustrations will be taken from Isaiah 55 and John 17. The reader is urged to become thoroughly acquainted with these chapters in order that the illustrations may be most effective.

(1) Definitive or Explanatory Question

(a) Term-al Question

In John 17:1 Jesus asks that the Father glorify His Son. Simply to note the presence of the term "glorify" is not sufficient. One must further ask these or similar questions: "What is meant by the term 'glorify' in this particular context? What is involved in Jesus' being glorified?" Every non-routine term should be similarly subjected to explanatory questions; for unless this is done, terms will become ends in themselves instead of means to an end, symbols through which to grasp realities.[12]

(b) Structural Question

One may observe that verses 8-9 of Isaiah 55 employ the structural relations of ideological contrast and comparison. God's thoughts and ways are contrasted to man's thoughts and ways, and this contrast is compared with the contrast between the heavens and the, earth. Merely to observe that there are logical contrasts and comparisons in these verses is not synonymous with fathoming the depths of the author's mind. Such observations do involve the noting of grammatical structure, which is the means of communication and therefore the means of interpretation. But there is more than structural form in this passage; there is structural content which is being conveyed by the form. So one should ask these definitive questions: "What is meant by contrasting God's ways and thoughts to man's? Wherein are God's ways and thoughts actually different from man's? Wherein do the heavens and earth differ, and how is this difference similar to that between God's thoughts and ways and man's?"

It will be noted that the answers to these structural questions will depend on the answers to certain term-al questions growing out of the observation of "thoughts," "ways," "heaven," and "higher." Further, they will depend upon noting the structural relation between verses 8-9 and those which precede, namely, verses 6-7, and asking the proper structural questions on the basis of this observation. One notices that verse 8 begins with a "for," thus indicating that the law of ideological substantiation is being utilized. Verses 8-9 provide a partial explanation of the reason for verses 6-7, which describe the effect. However, simply to see this connection is not enough. These questions must be asked and eventually answered: "For what idea in verses 6-7 do verses

8-9 provide the reason? Wherein do verses 8-9 actually provide the cause for this particular effect?"

Similarly, the observer notes the implicit presence of the law of ideological causation in John 17:4-5. Verse 4 contains the reason for verse 5. The following questions therefore naturally arise: "Wherein does that which is contained in verse 4 result in that which is found in verse 5? How is verse 5 the outcome of verse 4?" The answering of these questions will result in getting behind form to substance, in finding ideas through structure. Unless this is accomplished, observation is ultimately of no account.

Corresponding definitive questions may and should be asked in connection with all the other laws of structure in order that their meaning may be discerned. For example, the observation of the law of *generalization* or *particularization* ought to elicit such questions as these: "Wherein are the particulars illustrations of the general principle? How is the general principle elucidated by the specific examples?" The observation of *instrumentation* should educe queries like these: "Wherein is this a means to this end? How may or must this purpose be realized through this means?" Noting the law of *interrogation* should result in these questions: "How does this reply answer this question? Wherein is this question answered by this reply?" Observing the relation of *preparation* or *introduction* should evoke the following inquiries: "In what manner does this prepare one for an understanding of what follows? How is what follows illuminated by what precedes?" Seeing the law of *harmony* should provoke these questions: "What agreement is there between this and that? How does this solution meet this need? Wherein is this a fulfilment of the promise given? How do these elements dovetail?" Noticing the law of *cruciality* should lead to such questions as these: "How does this event cause this change? How would the passage be different if this event had not occurred?" The observation of *climax* should result in these inquiries: "Wherein is this a climax for the rest of the passage? How does the remainder of the passage lead up to this climax?" Seeing the law of *summarization* in operation should elicit these questions: "In what ways does this summarize the rest of the material? How is the summary substantiated by the remainder of the passage?" Similar questions can and should be asked in relation to the other laws of composition.

The reader is urged to study the passages given as illustrations of the laws of relationship in the discussion of structural observation and practice raising the explanatory questions which correspond with those which have been suggested above. He should not be concerned about using the same terminology, since these questions may be adapted and particularized in view of the Scriptural unit involved. The important thing is to be sure that they will result in seeing the meaning of the structural forms observed. One should also be certain that one asks explanatory questions with understanding and not simply as an exercise, since the rote asking of them will not be of any benefit in achieving a profound understanding of the realities which underlie the literary symbols of the Scriptures.

(c) Form-al Question

We now proceed to an investigation of the definitive question as it relates to the observation of general literary forms. In this instance the explanatory question has as its primary function the precise definition of literary forms. For example, when one ascertains that a certain portion utilizes the poetic form, these explanatory questions should be raised: "What is meant by the poetic form? What are its characteristics? What distinguishes it from other forms? Wherein does this portion consist of poetry?" By asking and answering such questions the interpreter will be delivered from a cursory characterization of the literary form of a passage without realizing the meaning and significance of that characterization.

These questions are applicable as well to the other literary forms previously discussed.[18] It must be remembered that in the case of explanatory form-al questions, there is not the need that all of them be repeated continually as in the cases of term-al and structural questions. For once one has mastered the answer to the question, "What exactly is meant by the particular literary forms?" one will find it unnecessary to ask the same question repeatedly. This applies also to the explanatory atmospheric question, which will now be considered.

(d) Atmospheric Question

Explanatory atmospheric questions purpose to find the meaning of the terms used to describe the underlying tone of passages and to discover wherein the passages reveal the mood ascribed to them. Consequently, when one employs terms like "joy," "urgency," "confident assurance," "contriteness," or "humility" to delineate a portion of Scripture, one should ask: "What is the precise meaning of this term? What elements constitute such a state or frame of mind? What aspects of the passage support such a description?" If this is done, then the observation of atmosphere will have its proper reward. Otherwise, it will be a meaningless operation which might better be left undone.[14]

(2) Rational Question [15]

This type of question corresponds to the second phase of interpretation, and its object is to discover the *general reasons* why certain Scriptural statements are made and the more *specific purposes* for their expression in a particular context and in a given historical situation. In view of this it is a key type of question; for it penetrates into the very recesses of the author's mind, the minds of the characters concerning whom he was writing, and the minds of the recipients of his writings. Biblical exposition will be greatly enhanced by the proper use of this kind of question.

The rational question is characterized by the interrogative "why." This is not to say that it cannot be expressed in other ways, but rather that the term "why" best conveys its inherent meaning. To illustrate wherein this is true, as well as its significance, the writer recalls an experience he had while traveling by train to a preaching appointment. Across the aisle sat a mother with her daughter, who was three or four years old. Like most children, this young girl showered her mother with questions. The questions were progressive in nature, each more difficult than the preceding one. First she asked observational questions: "What is this and what is that?" Then she proceeded to definitive questions: "What does this do, and what does that do?" Finally, she asked the most profound and troublesome type of question: *"Why* does this do what it does? *Why* does that do what it does?" In many cases the mother was able to answer the first two types of questions, but the answer to the third type often surpassed her knowledge. The young girl had discovered the true secret of learning, as children often do to the embarrassment of adults. And had her mother been able to answer all of her questions, especially those concerned with the "why" of things, the child would have received a liberal education by the time the train reached its destination.

The "why" question should be asked even if the reasons and motives for Biblical statements are not explicit; for they are always present when an intelligent being is at work. If they are not expressed they are implied, and they should be sought because they are of supreme importance in understanding the author's mind.

It is also important to realize that "why" questions are virtually inexhaustible. For each answer one gives may be subjected further to the same question, "Why?" Therein lies the secret of its tremendous power. Let the reader test this fact for himself and he will be thoroughly convinced of the importance of this type of interpretive question.

It now remains to give some concrete illustrations of how the rational question operates in connection with the various constituents of a passage.

(a) Term-al Question

In John 17:11 Jesus addresses God as "Holy Father." After noting the presence of the term "Holy" and after ascertaining its definition by answering the explanatory question, "What does it mean?" these further questions may be raised: "Why may God be called 'Holy'? Why did Jesus so address His Father at this time?" Likewise, when one has observed the term "consecrate" in John 17:17 and has inquired into its meaning, one should raise the following question: "Why did Jesus pray in this connection that the disciples be consecrated?"

(b) Structural Question

In Isaiah 55:1 the relative clause "that thirsteth" is used to qualify the subject "every one." After discovering the definitions of the terms employed in these expressions as well as the meaning of the relations between them, one should make this inquiry: "Why is 'every one' qualified by 'that thirsteth'?" Furthermore, the interpreter notes that "every one that thirsteth" is exhorted to come to the waters. When he has considered the explanations of the terms and relations in this expression, he must then ask himself: "Why is 'every one that thirsteth' asked to come to the waters?"

In the study of John 17 one notes that the laws of ideological causation, substantiation, and instrumentation are utilized to a great degree. The petitions stated in the prayer are either preceded or followed by the bases for them. Sometimes the relation between petition and reason is one of cause followed by effect, or causation, such as in verses 4-5; at other times it is effect followed by cause, or substantiation, such as in verses 10-11. In verse 21 their relation is one of means to end, or instrumentation. Further,

one observes that two-thirds of the prayer is devoted to the
reasons for the petitions and only one-third to the petitions
themselves. Thus there is quantitative selectivity in this
passage.[16] After one has observed the causes, effects, and
purposes, and has explained wherein the causes given have
the effects stated, and the means enable the ends to be
realized, one must then make these inquiries: "Why are
the laws of causation, substantiation, and instrumentation
used to such a degree in this passage? Why does Jesus devote
most of the prayer to the bases for the petitions rather than
to the petitions themselves?"

Also in the study of John 17 one notes a certain progression in the prayer which concerns those for whom the
petitions are made. First Jesus prays for Himself, then for
His immediate disciples, and finally for His future disciples.
In view of this development, the following rational question should be raised: "Why does Jesus begin with Himself,
and successively pray in behalf of His immediate disciples
and of His future Church?"[17]

It should be noted that under certain conditions rational
questions are partially answered by replying to explanatory
questions. For example, John 17:21 reads: "that they may
all be one; even as thou, Father, art in me, and I in thee,
that they also may be in us, so that the world may believe
that thou hast sent me." The basic structural relation in
this statement is that of ideological instrumentation. The
means is: "that they may all be one; even as thou, Father,
art in me, and I in thee, that they also may be in us." The
purpose is: "so that the world may believe that thou hast
sent me." On the basis of the observation of this structural
relation, the following explanatory questions may be asked:
"Wherein is the part of the statement designated 'means'
the actual avenue through which that which has been
termed 'purpose' realized?" To be more specific, "Wherein
does the oneness of believers with God and Christ and
with each other have as its purpose and result the world's

believing in Jesus' Divine commission?" The answers to
these explanatory questions will serve at least as a partial
reply to the rational questions, "Why was instrumentation
used in this instance and why did Jesus make this request
at this time?" Thus under certain circumstances the explanatory and rational questions overlap. Yet even in such instances the replies to rational questions may well transcend
those to definitive questions. Furthermore, in other cases
the two types of questions are more distinct. It is therefore
imperative that the interpreter learn to utilize both kinds of
questions.[18]

(c) Form-al and Atmospheric Questions [19]

In connection with *literary forms,* the over-all rational
question may be stated thus: "Why is this literary form
employed in general and why in this particular instance?"
This may be applied, for example, to the use of the parabolic form in the Gospels.[20]

The following rational question may be raised on the
basis of the observation and explanation of *atmosphere:*
"Why does this kind of atmosphere dominate this particular
passage?"

(3) Implicational Question

This type of question generally forms the last major
ripple resulting from the casting of an observation into the
sea of thought. In fact, it is actually an expansion of the
rational question, and its answer begins forming the bridge
between interpretation and application. First there is observation, answering the question, "What is here?" Then follows the definitive question, "What does it mean?" This
is succeeded by the question of reason, "Why is this particular thing with this particular meaning true and why is
it here?" Finally, there is the implicational question, "What
are the full implications of this particular thing with this
particular meaning placed here for these particular reasons?"

(a) Term-al Question

In John 17 the interpreter notes several uses of the term "one" in relation to the disciples. Having ascertained its meaning and the reasons for its inclusion, he must further seek the answer to this question: "What are the full implications of Jesus' prayer for the oneness of the disciples?"

(b) Structural Question

In Isaiah 55:7 the law of ideological causation is implicit. The cause is in the form of an exhortation: "let the wicked forsake his way, and the unrighteous man this thoughts; and let him return unto Jehovah." The result is: "and he will have mercy upon him." The question which arises following the answers to the explanatory and rational questions is this: "What is the complete significance of the fact that merciful pardon results from the wicked's forsaking his way and returning to Jehovah?"

(c) Form-al and Atmospheric Questions

The general *form-al* question is: "What are the various implications of a particular literary form, such as the dramatic or parabolic form?" [21]

The general *atmospheric* question is: "What is the full significance of the presence of this atmosphere in this passage?"

(4) Identifying, Modal, Temporal, and Local Questions

These four types of questions may be classified together in that they form a group subordinate to the preceding three. They are subservient because in a real sense their replies are involved in the answers to the other three types, although at times they make a distinct contribution by pointing up certain specific factors which might have been overlooked in answering the more general questions. In fact, they sometimes serve to answer the observational question, "What is here?"

Of the four mentioned in this category, the modal question is probably the most significant. Furthermore, one should note that all of these questions are not applicable to all the constituents of a passage. They are mainly relevant in regard to terms and structure.

(a) Identifying Question

Term-al—In Isaiah 55:4 are found the terms "him," "witness," "peoples," "leader," and "commander." This question is pertinent: "Exactly who is meant by each of these terms?"

Structural—Isaiah 55:5 contains this expression: "a nation that thou knowest not." One may ask, "What is the identity of this 'nation' in view of the structural connection involved in this statement and adjoining relations?"

(b) Modal Question

This type of question, like the implicational question, often forms the bridge between interpretation and application.

Term-al—The term "keep" is used in John 17:11. The modal question could be expressed thus: "In what specific ways is what is meant by this term accomplished? How does God 'keep'?"

Structural—There is an ideological comparison between the fulfilment of the purpose of the rain and snow and the realization of the intent of God's word in Isaiah 55:10-11. One should ask, "How is this comparison actualized and therefore justifiable?"

(c) Temporal and Local Questions

Term-al—In John 17:1 Jesus asks His Father to glorify His Son. The temporal and local questions would be: "When and where does what is meant by 'glorify' materialize?"

Structural—In relation to the contrast of Isaiah 55:13, one may inquire, "When and where is what is involved in this contrast to be realized?"

b. *General Illustration of Interpretive Questions*

In order further to clarify what is entailed in the formulation and function of interpretive questions, there will follow an illustration of how the process operates in relation to a given passage, in this instance Psalm 23.[22] In one column will be placed some of the observations made on the Psalm, and in another column the questions to which the observations give rise.

The forthcoming illustration should be especially beneficial in helping the reader to distinguish between the various types of interpretive questions and thus better qualify him to understand their use and significance. In order to facilitate the accomplishment of this purpose, the following system will be employed to classify the questions. If a question is observational in nature, it will be marked with an *O*.[23] If the question is interpretive, it will be marked in the following ways in order to indicate the phase of interpretation which it represents: *D* for definitive, *R* for rational, *IMP* for implicational, *ID* for identifying, *M* for modal, *T* for temporal, and *L* for local. Components of the passage with which the questions are concerned will be designated by these symbols: *t* for terms, *s* for structure, *f* for literary form, and *a* for atmosphere. Here is an example: an interpretive question concerned with the definition of a term will be marked *D-t*.

Observations	Interpretive Questions
(1) V. 1a—"Jehovah is my shepherd"—The name "Jehovah" is used for Deity instead of another name or title.	(1) What is the meaning of "Jehovah"? (*D-t*) Why is it used instead of another name for Deity, such as "God"? (*R-t*)

OBSERVATIONS	INTERPRETIVE QUESTIONS
(2) V. 1a—Jehovah is likened to a shepherd.	(2) What are the characteristics, attitudes, and functions of a shepherd? (D-t) Why is Jehovah described as a shepherd? (R-s) [24] What are the fuller implications of the use of this description? (IMP-s)
(3) V. 1a—"Shepherd" is qualified by the possessive pronoun "my." The Psalm does not say a shepherd, but my shepherd.	(3) What is involved in the relationship implied by the "my"? (D-s) Why this emphasis on personal possession? (R-s)
(4) V. 1a—The use of the expression "my shepherd" implies that the writer classified himself as one of the Sheep.[25]	(4) What is the nature of a Sheep? (D-t) What is a Sheep's relation to the Shepherd? (D-s) Why does a Sheep need a Shepherd? (R-s)
(5) V. 1a—The Psalm begins with a positive and unequivocal declaration—"Jehovah is my shepherd." This statement contains no "ifs" or "buts." It does not say "I hope" or "I wish." It is a statement of assurance and certainty. It says, in effect, "It is a present reality beyond question of doubt that Jehovah is my shepherd."	(5) Why does the Psalmist begin with this declaration of fact? (R-s) What are the implications of such a beginning? (IMP-s)
(6) V. 1b—"I shall not want" —The subject is not Jehovah but "I." Because something is true of Jehovah, something is also true of the Psalmist. This "I" corresponds with the "my" of the first clause. The verse does not read, "Jehovah is your shepherd, I shall not want."	(6) Why the correspondence between "my" and "I"? (R-s) What is the full significance of this correspondence? (IMP-s)

OBSERVATIONS

(7) V. 1—"Shall not want" is in the future tense, whereas "is" in the preceding clause is in the present. The second clause might have read, "I do not want."

(8) V. 1b—The Psalmist says, "I shall not *want*." He does not say, "I shall not need" or "I shall lack nothing."

(9) There is no expressed connection between the two parts of v. 1. Their relation is implicit in their thought-content and position. That relation seems to be one of ideological causation: Jehovah is my shepherd, therefore I shall not want.

(10) Note the movement from the positive to the negative in v. 1. Jehovah *is*—I shall *not*. The Psalmist could have written, "Jehovah is my shepherd, I shall have everything."

(11) V. 2a—"He maketh me to lie down in green pastures." The subject is in the third per-

INTERPRETIVE QUESTIONS

(7) Does the future include the present? (*D-t*) Why the progression from the present to the future? (*R-s*) Why not use the simple present in the second clause? (*R-t*)

(8) What is the import of the term "want"? (*D-t*) Is it synonymous with "desire"? (*D-t*) How inclusive a term is it; does it involve both physical and spiritual want? (*D-t*) Why not use another term, such as "need"? (*R-t*)

(9) Is this the true relation between the two parts? (*O*) If so, what is its meaning; wherein does the fact stated in the first part result in that stated in the second part, and wherein is the effect an outgrowth of the cause? (*D-s*) Why does the Psalmist employ this relation of cause and effect? (*R-s*) What are its various implications? (*IMP-s*)

(10) Why does the writer employ the negative rather than the positive? (*R-s*)

(11) What is the significance of this alternation of pronouns referring to the Psalmist and

OBSERVATIONS

son and is similar to the subject of v. 1a. Further, it is in contrast to the first person "I," which is the subject of v. 1b. As one scans the remainder of the passage in view of this, one discovers an alternation between "He" and "I," as well as the use of the second person for Deity instead of the third person (see v. 4). This in turn leads to the observation of the strong personal tone of the Psalm.

(12) V. 2a—"Maketh" seems to imply the element of coercion.

(13) V. 2a—"Maketh" is qualified by "to lie down" and "in green pastures," indicating the *what* and the *where* of the action of the verb. These terms are figurative and continue the image of the shepherd with which the Psalm begins.

(14) There is no explicit relation between verses 1 and 2. Vs. 2ff. may involve either the ideological particularization of v. 1 or its ideological substan-

INTERPRETIVE QUESTIONS

Deity? (*IMP-s*) Why change from second to third person in connection with Jehovah? (*R-s*) Why is there such a strong personal note throughout the Psalm? (*R-s*)

(12) Does this verb involve coercion? (*D-t*) What is the sense of the verb? (*D-t*)

(13) What is the connotation of the expression "to lie down," especially in the figurative sense? (*D-s*) Why does Jehovah, like a shepherd, make His Sheep "to lie down"? (*R-s*) What are pastures? (*D-t*) What are green pastures? (*D-t*) Why "lie down" instead of "eat"? (*R-t*) In what concrete ways is the statement realized that Jehovah makes the Psalmist to lie down in green pastures? (*M-s*)

(14) Which of these relations is valid? (*O*) Is there a possibility of combining elements in both of them? (*O*) If the relation involves the movement

OBSERVATIONS

tiation. In the first case the Psalmist would be saying, "Because Jehovah is my shepherd, I shall not want; and what I mean by not wanting is that I will be made to lie down in green pastures," etc. In the second instance he would be implying, "Because Jehovah is my shepherd, I shall not want; for he makes me to lie down in green pastures," etc. In this connection note the movement from the future tense in v. 1b to the present in v. 2a.

(15) There is no explicit relation between the two parts of v. 2. However, the fact that the second part has the same subject as the first, namely, "He," suggests that the element of extension is present. The clause "He leadeth me beside the still waters" seems to continue a description of the specific activities of Jehovah-Shepherd. In fact, "He" as a subject continues through v. 3.

(16) V. 2b—The verb is "leadeth," which seems to suggest a contrast to the idea of being driven.

(17) V. 2b—"Beside the still waters" indicates where the

INTERPRETIVE QUESTIONS

from the general to the specific, wherein is the general explicated by the specific and wherein are the specific statements an explanation of the general one? (D-s) If the relation is one of conclusion followed by reasons, wherein is the conclusion an outgrowth of the causes, and in what ways do the causes make possible the conclusion? (D-s) Why the movement from the future to the present tense? (R-s)

(15) What do these facts contribute to the discovery of the structure of the Psalm? (O) What is the essence of the structural factors thus discovered? (D-s)

(16) What is involved in the Shepherd's leading the Psalmist? (M-s) Why does the Shepherd "lead" instead of "drive"? (R-s) What are the fuller implications of this fact? (IMP-s)

(17) Why is "beside" used in this connection rather than

OBSERVATIONS

Psalmist is led. Note that "beside" is used instead of "to," which might be expected. The marginal reading for "still waters" is "waters of rest."

(18) V. 2—Thus far the Psalmist seems to have suggested that the basic needs of Sheep are met by the Divine Shepherd: pasturage, rest, and water. These were not easy to find in Palestine.

(19) V. 3—"He restoreth my soul: He guideth me in the paths of righteousness for his name's sake"—This verse contains more literal terms than the preceding ones.

(20) There is a question as to the relation of v. 3a to what precedes, for no connection is expressed.

(21) V. 3a—The object of "restoreth" is not "body" but "soul."

INTERPRETIVE QUESTIONS

"to"? (R-s) What is the difference between the marginal reading and that of the text proper? (D-t and s) Is the word translated "still" a description of the quality of the waters, the effect of the waters, or both? (D-s) Whichever is true, why should the Shepherd lead His Sheep "beside the still waters"? (R-s)

(18) If true, what is the full significance of these facts? (IMP-s)

(19) Why this resort to more literal terms in v. 3? (R-t and s)

(20) What is the relation between v. 3a and what precedes? (O) Is v. 3a the result of v. 2, or is it parallel to v. 2? (O) Whichever it may be, what is meant by their relation? (D-s)

(21) What is meant by "restoreth"? (D-t) What is the definition of "soul"? (D-t) Is it the same or different from "spirit"? (D-t) Why does the Psalmist

|

use "soul" instead of another term, such as "body"? (*R-t*) What may the use of this term indicate concerning the relation of v. 3a to what precedes? (*O*) Why does the Shepherd restore the Psalmist's soul? (*R-s*) In what specific ways is such a restoration accomplished? (*M-s*)

(22) V. 3b—"He guideth me in the paths of righteousness for his name's sake"—"Guideth" is used as distinguished from "leadeth" of v. 2b.

(22) What is meant by "guideth"? (*D-t*) Is it synonymous with "leadeth," or is it different? (*D-t*) Why does the Shepherd guide His Sheep? (*R-s*)

(23) V. 3b—"Guideth" is qualified by three prepositional phrases. The first two, "in the paths of righteousness," indicate the *direction* of the guidance; the third, "for his name's sake," denotes the *reason* for the guidance.

(23) What is the meaning of these structural relations? (*D-s*) What are their implications? (*IMP-s*)

(24) V. 3b—"Paths" is plural rather than singular.

(24) Why is the term "paths" used in this connection, both literally and figuratively? (*R-t*) What is the reason for its being plural, if any? (*R-t*)

(25) V. 3b—The paths in which the Psalmist is guided are described as "paths of righteousness."

(25) What is being conveyed by the term "righteousness"? (*D-t*) What is the purpose for guidance in the "paths of righteousness"? (*R-s*) Whose righteousness is it? (*ID-t*) Does "of righteousness" simply indicate

OBSERVATIONS

INTERPRETIVE QUESTIONS

a characteristic of the paths, namely, that they are righteous, or does it also indicate the goal of the paths, namely, paths leading to righteousness, or paths by which one may become righteous? (*D-s*) Are there other alternatives? (*D-s*) What are the implications of whichever definition is valid? (*IMP-s*)

(26) V. 3b—"For his name's sake" denotes the motivation for the guidance in the paths of righteousness. The antecedent of "his" is Jehovah-Shepherd. "Name's sake" may well read "sake of name," which calls attention to the term "sake." The purpose for the guidance mentioned therefore concerns Jehovah and more specifically His name. The passage does not say, "for the sheep's sake," which might normally be expected.

(26) What is the definition of "sake"? (*D-t*) What is meant by "name"? (*D-t*) Why is "name" used instead of another term, such as "own"? (*R-t*) Wherein does the sake of His name provide a motivation or purpose for guidance in the paths of righteousness? (*D-s*) What are the broader implications of the fact inherent in this structural relation? (*IMP-s*)

(27) No relation between v. 3b and v. 3a is expressed. One wonders if v. 3b is parallel to v. 3a or whether it involves progression. If there is progression, it may entail ideological instrumentation: "He restores my soul to the end that he may guide me in the paths of righteousness for his name's sake"; or, "Because he wants to guide me, he restores me."

(27) What is the relation between these clauses? (*O*) Is the law of instrumentation being employed? (*O*) If this be the structural relation, what is its meaning? (*D-s*)

OBSERVATIONS

(28) V. 4a—"Yea, though I walk through the valley of the shadow of death"—The intensive connective "yea" is used to begin this statement. This is the first connective utilized to relate clauses. The absence of expressed connections at the beginning of preceding clauses makes this stand out by contrast.

(29) V. 4a—"Walk" describes incomplete action and may therefore refer both to the present and future. This is true of some of the other verbs of v. 4.

(30) V. 4a—A series of three prepositional phrases is used to describe "walk": first, the local adverbial phrase "through the valley," indicating the direction or place of the walk; second, the adjectival phrase "of the shadow," qualifying the term "valley"; and third, the adjectival phrase "of death," qualifying the term "shadow." Both the latter phrases define the valley. Note the marginal reading "deep darkness," which combines these two phrases.

INTERPRETIVE QUESTIONS

(28) What is conveyed by the emphatic connection "yea"? (D-s) Why does the Psalmist use this kind of connection at this juncture? (R-s)

(29) What is signified by the term "walk," especially in the figurative sense? (D-t) Why is this tense used here? (R-t)

(30) What is denoted by the preposition "through"? (D-t) Why is "through" used instead of another preposition, such as "in"? (R-s) Further, what is a "valley"? (D-t) Why is "valley" used in this connection? (R-s) What is a "shadow"? (D-t) Why is it used in this connection? (R-s) Is "death" to be taken literally or figuratively? (D-t) What is involved in the relation between "shadow" and "death"? (D-s) What does an awareness of the marginal reading contribute to an understanding of the expression "the shadow of death"? (D-s) Is the phrase "of death" used to im-

ply the worst kind of shadow, the most extreme case, the most fearful of darknesses? (R-s)

(31) It is possible that the relation between v. 3b and v. 4a is that of ideological particularization. In other words, "the valley of deep darkness" may be one of the "paths of righteousness," and "walk" may include being "guided" by Jehovah-Shepherd.

(31) Is this the true connection involved in the movement between vs. 3 and 4? (O) If so, what is being conveyed by such a relation? (D-s) Why does a Shepherd lead His Sheep through the valley of deepest darkness? (R-s) What are the full implications of the law of particularization here? (IMP-s) [26]

(32) V. 4b—"I will fear no evil"—This is the independent clause to which the preceding clause is subordinate. The author is saying, "In spite of the circumstances described in the preceding clause, this will be true."

(32) What is the meaning of the structural relation between these two clauses? (D-s)

(33) V. 4b—The object of "will fear" is "evil," which is qualified by the negative "no," implying absolute negation: no evil whatsoever. Note also that the Psalmist does not say that there will be no evil present, but that no evil which is present will be feared.

(33) What is "fear"? (D-t) What is "evil"? (D-t) Why is fearing evil even suggested by the Psalmist? (R-s) What is meant by "fearing no evil" in the situation described in v. 4a? (D-s) What is the full significance of the fact that the Psalmist does not suggest the absence of evil, but the absence of fear? (IMP-s)

(34) V. 4b and c—"I will

(34) What is the exact re-

OBSERVATIONS

fear no evil" is substantiated by two reasons: "for thou art with me," and "thy rod and thy staff, they comfort me." These could involve parallel reasons, or the second could be a particularization of the first. In the former instance the connection might be expressed as follows: "I will fear no evil both because thou art with me and because thy rod and thy staff, they comfort me." In the latter instance, the sense might be stated in the following way: "I will fear no evil because thou art with me, and being with me, dost use thy rod and thy staff to comfort me."

(35) V. 4b—"thou art with me"—the antecedent of "thou" is Jehovah-Shepherd. The antecedent of "me" is the "I" which is the subject of both the preceding clauses. The relation between "thou" and "me" is expressed by the copula "art" and the preposition "with." "Art" is in the present tense, whereas the preceding verb "will fear" is in the future.

(36) V. 4c—"Thy rod and thy staff"—Note the repetition

INTERPRETIVE QUESTIONS

lation between the two clauses used as substantiations for the lack of fear for evil? (O) What is the author attempting to convey by such a relation? (D-s)

(35) What is expressed by "art with"? (D-t) In what sense can the Psalmist say that Jehovah-Shepherd is with him? (D-s) What reason is there, if any, for putting the verb "art" in the present whereas the verb "will fear" of the preceding clause is in the future? (R-s) Why does the author suggest this as a reason for his lack of fear? (R-s) What are the broader implications of the structural relation used here? (IMP-s)

(36) Why the repetition of the "thy"? (R-s) What is a

OBSERVATIONS	INTERPRETIVE QUESTIONS
of "thy." Observe also the use of the two terms "rod" and "staff."	"rod"? (*D-t*) What is a "staff"? (*D-t*) Are they the same or are they different? (*D-s*) Why does the author mention both "rod" and "staff"? (*R-s*)
(37) V. 4c—"they comfort me"—The element of redundancy appears here. "They," whose antecedents are the "rod" and "staff," is expressed although it is not needed. The verb which denotes the action of both rod and staff is "comfort."	(37) Why is "they" expressed although it does not seem to be needed? (*R-t*) What is meant by the verb "comfort"? (*D-t*) How do the "rod" and "staff" of Jehovah-Shepherd "comfort" the Psalmist? (*M-s*) Wherein does such "comfort" remove the fear of evil? (*D-s*)
(38) V. 5a—"Thou preparest a table before me in the presence of mine enemies"—The antecedent of "Thou" is Jehovah, but it no longer seems to be Jehovah-Shepherd, since a shepherd does not prepare a table for his sheep. The image seems to have changed to that of a host. This implies that the Psalmist is Jehovah's honored guest.	(38) Is the observation that there is a change of imagery from shepherd to host valid? (*O*) If so, why the change? (*R-s*) Are there any similarities or differences between a shepherd and a host? (*D-s*) Is the change one of form only or of content as well? (*D-s*) What is the relation of the ideas of vs. 5ff. to those of vs. 1-4? (*O*) What is involved in a host's preparing a table? (*D-s*) What is signified by Jehovah's preparing a table for the Psalmist? (*D-s*) Specifically how is this accomplished? (*M-s*) In what sense is it true that Jehovah is Host and the Psalmist His honored Guest? (*D-s*) What are the wider implications of this Host-Guest relationship? (*IMP-s*)

OBSERVATIONS	INTERPRETIVE QUESTIONS

(39) V. 5a—A series of two prepositional phrases is used to indicate the *locale* of the table's preparation: first, "before me" —the table is prepared in the presence of the Psalmist; and second, "in the presence of mine enemies"—not only in the presence of the Psalmist but, what is more amazing, also in the presence of the Psalmist's enemies.

(39) Who are the Psalmist's "enemies"? (*D-s*) Why should the Psalmist have enemies? (*R-s*) What is meant by Jehovah's preparing a table for the Psalmist in the presence of his enemies? (*D-s*) Why does the Psalmist suggest that Jehovah would do such a thing? (*R-s*)

(40) V. 5b—"Thou hast a- nointed my head with oil"— This seems to contain another action of Jehovah-Host. Not only does Jehovah prepare a table, but He also has anoint- ed the Psalmist's head with oil. "Preparest" is in the pres- ent tense, whereas "hast a- nointed" is in the present per- fect.

(40) What is meant by "a- nointed"? (*D-t*) What is "oil"? (*D-t*) Why does Jehovah-Host "anoint"? (*R-s*) Why does He anoint the "head"? (*R-s*) Why does He anoint the head with "oil"? (*R-s*) Why the change in tense noted in the observation? (*R-s*) What is involved in the relation between v. 5b and v. 5a? (*D-s*)

(41) V. 5c—"My cup runneth over"—It would seem as if this clause properly belongs after v. 5a, and yet it comes after v. 5b. Observe also the tense of the Psalmist's statement that his cup *is* running over. It is in the simple present, in con- trast to the present perfect of "hast anointed." Further, the statement does not merely de- note that the cup is full, but that it is full to overflowing.

(41) What is the purpose of a "cup"? (*D-t*) Why a "cup" in this connection? (*R-s*) What is signified by his cup's running over? (*D-s*) Why is his cup made to run over instead of simply being filled? (*R-s*) Why the change in tense from the present perfect to the simple present? (*R-s*) What is the re- lation between the statement about the anointing and the one about the cup? (*O*) Why

OBSERVATIONS

(42) There seem to be certain parallels between the images of the shepherd and host. For example, there is the similarity between the "green pastures" of v. 2 and the "table" of v. 5. Further, there seems to be a likeness between the "deep darkness" and "evil" of v. 4 and the "enemies" of v. 5, as well as between the "fearing no evil" of v. 4 and the preparing of a "table before me in the presence of mine enemies" of v. 5.

(43) V. 6a—"Surely goodness and lovingkindness shall follow me"—The marginal reading for the emphatic "surely" is "only." It is the second emphatic term used in the Psalm, the first being the "yea" of v. 4. "Goodness" and "lovingkindness" seem to be personified. "Shall follow" is in the future tense, although it also seems to involve the present.

INTERPRETIVE QUESTIONS

does the latter follow the former? (R-s) Is there any connection between the anointing and the running over; if so, what is it? (O) Why does the author utilize it? (R-s)

(42) Is this a valid observation? (O) If so, why are these parallels employed? (R-s)

(43) How are "surely" and "only" similar and different? (D-t) Which more nearly fits the thought here? (O) What is the full force of the emphatic "surely" or "only," whichever is here? (D-s) Why does the Psalmist use it in this connection? (R-s) What is the definition of "goodness"? (D-t) What is "lovingkindness"? (D-t) How are they related? (O) Why does the Psalmist use each one? (R-s) Why does he use both? (R-s) Whose "goodness" and "loving-

OBSERVATIONS	INTERPRETIVE QUESTIONS

kindness" are they? (*ID-s*) What is the essence of the term "follow"? (*D-t*) In what ways do "goodness and lovingkindness follow" the Psalmist? (*M-s*) Why the apparent personification? (*R-s*) Why is "shall follow" in the future tense? (*R-t*)

(44) There seems to be an implicit contrast between v. 6a and v. 5. Instead of the enemies of the Psalmist following or pursuing him, it is "goodness" and "lovingkindness" which follow him. Note the elements of contrast and causation which seem to be present when one relates the fact that the Psalmist follows the leading of Jehovah-Shepherd in vs. 2-3, and is followed by "goodness and lovingkindness" in v. 6. There is a progression from "follower" to "followed."

(44) Are these relations between v. 6a and what precedes valid? (*O*) If not, what are the relations? (*O*) What is involved in the use of these relations? (*D-s*)

(45) V. 6a—"all the days of my life"—Here are two prepositional phrases together indicating a temporal qualification of "shall follow." They answer the question, "How long?" Further, they answer the question unqualifiedly. The Psalmist does not say, "Most of my days," or "Almost all of my days."

(45) Why does the Psalmist so qualify "shall follow"? (*R-s*)

OBSERVATIONS	INTERPRETIVE QUESTIONS
(46) V. 6b—"And I shall dwell in the house of Jehovah for ever"—The connective between the two parts of v. 6 is "and." "Shall dwell" is in the future tense, although it also may embrace the present. "In the house of Jehovah" indicates the *locale* for the action of the verb. "For ever" connotes its *duration*. The marginal reading for the latter phrase is "for length of days." Note that the time element suggested is virtually unlimited. Observe also the apparent similarity between the "for ever" of v. 6b and "all the days of my life" of v. 6a.	(46) What is the relation to the preceding clause suggested by the "and"? (*O*) What is involved in this relation? (*D-s*) What is the import of the term "dwell"? (*D-t*) Why the future tense? (*R-t*) What is the "house of Jehovah"? (*D-s*) Why dwell in the house of Jehovah? (*R-s*) Why does the Psalmist state that he will dwell in the house of Jehovah "for ever"? (*R-s*) Wherein are the "for ever" of v. 6b and "all the days of my life" in v. 6a similar or different? (*O*) Why such similarities or differences? (*R-s*)
(47) There is a problem as to the relation of v. 6 to v. 5 and to the remainder of the Psalm.	(47) What is the relation of v. 6 to v. 5? (*O*) Is the image of the host continued in v. 6 or is it suspended at the end of v. 5? (*O*) What is the meaning of the relation of v. 6 to v. 5? (*D-s*) What is the relation of v. 6 to the Psalm as-a-whole? (*O*) Is it a summary of the whole, or is it another particular involved in the amplification of the thesis of v. 1? (*O*) Or does it form a climax in regard to the movement of the whole? (*O*) Is its relation to the Psalm as-a-whole different from its connection to v. 5? (*O*)

OBSERVATIONS	INTERPRETIVE QUESTIONS
	What is the purport of its relation to the whole? (D-s)
(48) The Psalm seems to contain these three primary elements: the character of Jehovah and His relation to the Psalmist; the actions of Jehovah growing out of His character and relation to the Psalmist; and the results of those actions in the experience of the Psalmist.	(48) Is such an analysis valid? (O) If so, why are these three elements utilized in the Psalm? (R-s) What are the implications of their presence and use? (IMP-s)
(49) There appear to be no definite indications of time and place in the Psalm. The only positive indication of the specific identity of the Psalmist is the title of the Psalm, "The Psalm of David."	(49) Who is the antecedent of the pronouns in the first person? (ID-t) When and where were these words spoken? (T and L) [27]
(50) The atmosphere of the Psalm may be described in various ways: calm assurance, quiet confidence, perfect rest, joyful trust.	(50) What is involved in such descriptions? (D-a) How are they carried out in the Psalm? (M-a) What are their implications? (IMP-a)
(51) The Psalm is one of experience. It is based on both past and present realization and it reaches out with statements concerning future expectations. The statements about the future are always grounded on past and present actualities. The reader may trace this fact throughout the Psalm.	(51) Why does the Psalmist base his expectations regarding the future on past and present experience? (R-s) What are the widespread implications of this connection? (IMP-s)

OBSERVATIONS	INTERPRETIVE QUESTIONS
(52) The Psalmist employs the poetic literary form to express his thoughts.	(52) Wherein is it true that Psalm 23 is poetry? (D-f) Why does the Psalmist use the poetic form to express himself? (R-f) How does an awareness of the poetic form of Psalm 23 enable one better to interpret it? (M-f) [28]

In order to answer some of the questions which probably arose in the reader's mind regarding this exercise, and in order to avoid any misunderstandings concerning it, there follows a list of explanatory statements which the reader is urged to note carefully.

First, it should not be assumed that this illustration exhausts the potentialities of the twenty-third Psalm. Rather, it represents some of the *elemental* observations and questions which may be noted in its study.

Second, this demonstration was based on the use of the American Revised Version. Reference to the Hebrew was purposely avoided in order to illustrate the firsthand study of the vernacular. Further, the project was limited to one translation for the sake of brevity. The reader may compare various translations and, if able, examine the original to make more observations.

Since this statement raises the question of the relation of the original to the vernacular in methodical study, it might be profitable to take a few moments to consider it at this place.

There are two main alternatives in this regard. One alternative is to place the translation and the original side by side as one observes, so that one may glance readily from one to the other. If such a practice is followed, it is usually best to treat the original as an aid to the study of the vernacular, and not the vernacular as an aid to the study of the original. That is, one's attention should be concentrated primarily on the translation. This suggestion is in keeping with the principle of direct study in the mother tongue.[29] One of the great values of this approach is that some observational errors will be avoided, especially in relation to the inflections of terms. The other alternative is to use only the translations in one's initial approach to a passage. This better enables one to realize the value of the vernacular, because one concentrates on it alone. In such a case one will not utilize the original until the phase of study is reached in which the interpretive questions are answered. Any errors which may have been made in the observational step can be corrected at that time. The reader is urged to adopt whichever practice best suits his own abilities and needs.

Third, there are some who may feel that the twenty-third Psalm, which is poetic in form, should not have been subjected to such a critical analysis. And they may be right. However, even poetry has its logic, its purposive selectivity, and its literary structure. Certainly good poetry is not illogical and without purpose. It is true that it appeals *primarily* to the emotions, as was stated heretofore;[30] but it is still an expression of mind. One must therefore attempt to keep the emotional and logical elements in balance in its interpretation.

Fourth, this exercise should not be used as an exact pattern to be copied in the formulation and recording of observations and interpretive questions. Each individual should develop the kind of procedure which is best accommodated to him. For example, the two column approach may not appeal to everyone for various reasons. One of these is that not everyone likes to list observations and interpretive questions simultaneously. This procedure appeals to the writer, because the questions are more meaningful and come to mind more readily when observations are fresh. However, others may find that another approach is more fruitful. If so, then by all means another approach should be used. The illustration from the twenty-third Psalm was meant to show how the interpretive questions arise from observations, and not to present an ideal model to be followed by all. This is substantiated by the fact that the writer himself often varies his approach.[31]

Fifth, it is not expected that the reader will immediately see the significance of all the observations and questions. In fact, even if their significance could be fully ascertained, one would find that they vary in importance. However, they all have some meaning; and if perchance this meaning is not clear at the outset and some of the observations and questions appear to be pointless, the reader is urged to make a serious attempt to understand their importance. For if he does, he will discover that his insight will grow and that they will increasingly take on more meaning. Often the reason for our failure to understand the signifiance of things lies not in the thing itself but in our own eyes.[32]

Sixth, the preceding exercise demonstrates the type of observation which begins with a detailed analysis of the parts and closes with a synthesis of the parts. In such an approach it is helpful to conclude one's observation by reading and rereading the whole so as to get its total effect. For there is the danger that one may fail to see the forest for the trees.[33]

Seventh, note that the observational process transcended mere physical sight. Although the words of the text were copied in order to make sure that the text was confronted by the eyes, to fix it in mind, and to have a basis for reference, the recording of observations did not end there. Statements were made about the text which promoted an awareness of its contents. Further, a certain amount of interpretation entered into the process. To be sure, when such interpretation went beyond that which was obvious, it was considered tentative. But it was present because its presence was involved in being aware. To summarize, the observational process was governed by two major considerations: it was so conducted as to be meaningful and worthwhile, and it was conducted in such a way as not to usurp the interpretive phase of inductive study.[34]

Eighth, in some instances grammatical analysis is purposely included so as to make the reader aware that it is inherent in the process of observation, although one may not engage in it consciously at all times.[35]

In this connection it should be stressed that grammatical analysis may be used in such a way so as to become an end rather than a means. This should be guarded against, for grammar is a servant and not a master. In fact, if the use of grammatical terminology is so burdensome that it attracts attention to itself and thereby hinders observation, it should by all means be discarded. One should utilize only those procedures which will serve as tools for enhancing one's perception.

Ninth, in the making of observations, the contrast between what the Psalm contained and what it did not contain was used at various times. Such a device is exceedingly helpful, since oftentimes one really sees what is included in a passage by consciously noting what is excluded from it.[36] Negative observation was also used in connection with noting the absence of explicit relations.

Tenth, the basic unit in observation was the clause. As a general practice, first the clause as-a-whole was noted, after which its various parts were observed. This is a practical procedure, since terms and phrases are not very meaningful apart from their relations within clauses. Furthermore, it helps to avoid the dissection of thought units into such small parts that their integrality is destroyed.

Eleventh, at times several observations were recorded in a group because of their relations to each other, and at other times observations were recorded individually. There is no hard and fast rule to guide one in deciding whether certain observations should be grouped together or listed separately. However, each person should make a conscious effort to discover that means of organizing and recording observations which will be most meaningful and permanently useful to him.[37]

Twelfth, though there was no thoroughgoing effort to label terms as routine or non-routine and literal or figurative, these classifications were utilized in the exercise. For example, routine terms were not given careful consideration.

Thirteenth, the classification of the questions is open to debate in some cases. This is especially true in relation to the distinction between term-al and structural questions. For though terms have a certain inherent content, they are so interrelated that it is sometimes difficult to think of them apart from their connections to each other. The reader should not be disturbed if he does not agree with some of the classifications or if he cannot understand a few of them. The basic purpose of the attempt to classify the questions was to call attention to the fact that the questions are concerned with the various components of a passage and to clarify the meaning and value of the different kinds of questions in relation to the phases of interpretation which they involve.

Fourteenth, some of the questions raised may be found to be unanswerable. The answers to others will not have great significance. However, these facts should not deter one from asking all the questions which come to mind. For one will discover, for example, that some questions which at the outset seem to be insignificant eventually become replete with meaning. It is a dangerous practice, therefore, to prejudge questions as to their possibilities and to include only those which at first glance seem to be answerable or important. Such a procedure may deprive one of some of the best insights into Biblical truth. In this case as in many others, it is better to be safe than sorry.

Fifteenth, expository questions should not be recorded cursorily or indiscriminately, for they will be meaningless unless they are done thoughtfully and with understanding. Therefore, if one does not have at least some glimmer as to their meaning and potentialities, one would do better not to utilize them.

In order to sharpen one's awareness of the possibilities of interpretive questions, it is recommended that one reread thoughtfully the preceding list of questions, making a studied attempt to discover their purpose and value. If the reader has already followed such a course, he should disregard this suggestion.

Sixteenth, the questions asked were adapted to particular observations. This was true in terms of the kind of questions used as well as their phraseology. In some instances definitive, rational, and implicational questions were all utilized. In others only definitive questions were employed, whereas on some occasions the definitive and rational phases of interpretation were combined in a rational question. The implicational question was used primarily in connection with some of the key thoughts of the passage. In all instances the nature of the observations which gave rise to the questions determined the kind used. Moreover, the terminology used in the questions was adapted to the observations on which they were based. For example, the general definitive question, "What does this mean?" when applied to a phrase of verse 2 was stated thus: "Is the word translated 'still' a description of the quality of the waters, the effect of the waters, or both?" Such an approach helps to particularize the question and thereby to focus one's thought. It also prevents one's becoming stereotyped and consequently cursory. Another good preventive in this connection is to find synonymous ways of expressing even the general questions. The reader probably noted how this was done in the exercise.[38]

Seventeenth, one may observe that some of the questions asked were redundant in certain respects. Sometimes a general question was asked, and it was followed by specific questions whose answers would be involved in a full reply to the general question. In some instances the same question was asked in different words. In addition, there is the fact that the various types of questions sometimes overlapped. And yet the asking of these questions in various forms in spite of this element of redundancy is purposeful and necessary because of the very nature of truth and of the human mind. Truth has so many facets and the mind is so limited in its ability to grasp them that one needs to bombard it from various angles in order to make possible a well-rounded insight into truth. What one does not discover in the answering of one question one may find in answering another. For this reason one should not be concerned in formulating only those questions which are mutually exclusive, even if it were possible to do so. It should be added, however, that meaningless repetition should also be avoided.

Eighteenth, it is not to be expected that all expository questions which will eventually be asked will be formulated in connection with the initial observational approach. For as was previously noted, one will not make certain observations until the process of interpretation is at least partially completed. Such observations will in turn give rise to corresponding interpretive questions. As a matter of fact, neither observation nor the formulation of questions can ever be completed. There will always remain observations to be made and expository questions to be asked.[39]

Nineteenth, it is not expected that the questions will be answered in the exact order in which they were raised. One will need to take into consideration the exercise as-a-whole and follow the order which is consistent with the demands of logic and of the passage. It may be that a question asked early in observation may need to be answered near the end of the interpretive process.

And in conclusion, the writer is aware that one cannot spend as much time on every passage as is required to make a complete list of observations and interpretive questions, although it is amazing how thoroughness in this regard often economizes time in the long run. The reader is urged to be as thoroughgoing as possible in these practices, since he will thereby develop certain abilities which will serve him well even when he cannot give as much time as he would like to the study of a given passage. For in the last analysis, the ability to observe and to formulate intelligently the questions of interpretation represents a major share of methodical study. If the reader develops along these lines, he will be well on his way to the achievement of his goal.

Exercise

Observe *fully* the following passages: Exodus 15:1-21, Joshua 1, Nehemiah 1, Psalm 121, Isaiah 6, 53, Matthew 4:1-11, 5:1-12, Mark 7:1-30, John 15:1-8, Acts 9:1-19a, Romans 3:21-31, Revelation 5.[40] Formulate *thorough* lists of interpretive questions on the basis of your observations. Classify each question as to the component of the passage and the phase of interpretation with which it is concerned. Keep in mind the suggestions of the preceding pages.

B. Interpretive Answers

Exegesis hinges not only on one's ability to ask the proper interpretive questions, but also on one's ability to make proper replies to them. For one's replies constitute interpretation proper.

1. Determinants of Interpretive Answers

The first problem which arises in discovering how to answer interpretive questions concerns finding the ingredients which determine what those answers shall be. In so doing one must remember that two primary factors are involved in exposition: the subject—the individual; and the object—the Scriptures. Thus the process of exegesis will be influenced by both subjective and objective elements.

An effort will now be made to list *all* of the *major* determinants, subjective and objective, which will account for the answer to *any* conceivable interpretive question.

a. *Subjective Determinants*

(1) Spiritual Sense

Since this factor is easily misunderstood, let it be clear at the outset that it does not directly concern the spiritual sense of the text in contrast to its literal sense. It involves the nature of the interpreter of the text rather than the nature of the text itself.

There is a moral and spiritual factor residing in the individual which inevitably enters into the process of interpretation. And, although it is intangible, it is just as real and probably more important than those elements which are objective and tangible. Paul had this principle in mind when he wrote: "The unspiritual man does not receive the gifts of the Spirit of God, for they are folly to him, and he is not able to understand them because they are spiritually discerned." (I Corinthians 2:14) Jesus was utilizing the same principle when He said to the Jews who, marvelling at His teaching, wondered as to its source: "My teaching is not mine, but his who sent me; if any man's will is to do his will, he shall know whether the teaching is from God or whether I am speaking on my own authority." (John 7:16-17) [41]

In view of this, Biblical exposition should never be conceived as a purely mechanical or intellectual process, for it engages the spirit of man as well. Thus, given the same aptitudes with regard to the techniques of exegesis, two persons will differ in their ability to understand Scriptural truth proportionately to their possession of spiritual sense. In fact, so important is the spiritual factor that one sometimes finds individuals who, though deficient in the skills of interpretation, far surpass in insight those who have had the best training in exegetical procedures.

Spiritual sense is made possible by the presence of certain characteristics. Among them are teachableness, sincerity, and an intimate knowledge of God. The more one possesses these, the more profound will be one's insight into Biblical truth. For they make possible receptivity to God's Spirit, who, having motivated and guided the experience of Scriptural authors, is also their best interpreter.[42]

(2) Common Sense

Though this ingredient is also subjective, it probably ranks second in importance only to the spiritual factor. Its significance lies in the fact that due to their attitude toward the Scriptures, many are overcome by a peculiar outlook which causes them to leave their common sense outside the door when they enter the sanctuary of Biblical interpretation. As a result they look for trick or magical explanations. They are not content to accept the obvious meaning of the text; they must find something sensational in it. Imagery is taken literally, and literal statements are construed figuratively. No place is allowed for the use of hyperbole. If the newspaper were read in this manner, the outcome would be disastrous.

The only antidote for these dangerous practices is to remind oneself of the need for plain common sense in the interpretation of the Scriptures. This is probably what Coleridge had in mind when he urged that the Bible be read like any other book. If this simple principle were conscientiously applied, many troublesome problems and faulty conclusions would be avoided.

This advice is especially needed in the interpretation of Jesus' teachings. It is often forgotten that Jesus, wise teacher that He was, sometimes made unqualified statements in order to approximate the truth and to make a forceful impress on the minds of His listeners. Such statements may be found, for example, in Matthew 5-7. It does not follow, however, that they admit of no exceptions. Jesus would be the first one to recognize this fact, because He had enough common sense to know the complications which confront men in real life situations. He merely did what other wise teachers do in similar circumstances, that is, He used what amounted to hyperbolic statements in order to emphasize certain much needed truths. This view represents a common sense approach to Jesus' teaching, as over against the approach which permits of no hyperbole in Jesus' words. It is such a use of common sense which is urged in this discussion.

It should be stressed that the principle of common sense, like every good thing, is capable of misapplication. It may become the means of lowering Divine standards to meet human standards. It may be used as an excuse for failing to heed Scriptural exhortations. However, the presence of these dangers ought not to hide the validity of the principle itself, and ought only to motivate one to be careful in its application.[43]

(3) Experience

Closely related to the preceding two factors is that of experience, which is important enough to warrant separate treatment. It is significant from various standpoints.

For one thing, the peculiarities of one's own experience are invariably reflected in the interpretive process. This principle is readily borne out by a study of the history of the Christian Church. Men with certain backgrounds and problems have always expounded Scriptural truths on the basis of their individual outlooks. Witness the interpretations of Origen and Augustine. Each person, then, comes to the Scriptures with a unique experience, and that experience cannot but influence his exposition of Biblical statements. This fact has both its values and its dangers, but it is unavoidable.

Moreover, one's understanding of the Scriptures is influenced by one's understanding of experience. For since the Scriptures are the expression of experience, they must be interpreted in the light of experience. Thus one discovers that the ability to analyze life in general often coincides with the ability to gain profound insights into the Scriptures, and vice versa.

It may be assumed that if Biblical statements are true, they will correspond with the facts of human existence and experience. If, then, certain interpretations contradict the observable data of life, then one ought at least to question them, if not discard them. One finds that such a comparison of Biblical interpretations with experience often serves as a helpful corrective to erroneous exegesis.

In view of these facts, it behooves one to become a careful and analytical observer of life. For the greater one's understanding of human experience, including one's own, the greater one's insight into the meaning of Biblical experience.

b. *Objective Determinants*

(1) Etymology, Usage, Synonyms, Comparative Philology, and Kind of Terms [44]

The *etymology* of terms includes two factors: their root meaning and their derivative significance. These factors cast much light on the definition of Biblical terms. Consider, for instance, *pasha'*, one of the words used in the Old Testament to describe sin. Its *root* meaning is to revolt or to refuse subjection to a rightful authority. It is found in its original sense in I Kings 12:19. From this root idea is *derived* the spiritual concept, which in view of its origin involves revolting or rebelling against God. The word is used in this sense in Isaiah 44:22. Therefore, by the employment of this term, sin is pictured as a personal, voluntary, irrational act of defiance against the rightful authority of the universe. An awareness of the root meaning and derivative significance of *pasha'* thus affords insights into the deeper connotations of sin than can often be gained through a translation.

There are various works which supply etymological information. Some of these are: Abbott-Smith, *A Manual Greek Lexicon of the New Testament;* Liddell and Scott, *A Greek-English Lexicon;* Thayer, *A Greek-English Lexicon of the New Testament;* Trench, *Synonyms of the New Testament;* Vincent, *Word Studies in the New Testament;* Gesenius, *Hebrew and English Lexicon;* and Girdlestone, *Synonyms of the Old Testament.* Bible dictionaries such as the *International Standard Bible Encyclopedia* and Hastings' *Dictionary of the Bible* are also helpful.

The interpreter should be warned against too great a dependence on etymological factors in interpretation, for Scriptural terms may at times be far removed from the original roots from which they sprang. As a result, if in those instances too much stress is placed on root meaning and derivation, misinterpretation is the consequence. Therefore, it should be remembered that there is another factor which may be even more important than etymology. This is the factor of the *usage* of words, both in Biblical and extra-Biblical writings.

The most important of these is Biblical usage. And even more significant is the way in which the author of a particular book or group of books utilizes a certain word. For it is unquestionably true that not all Biblical authors use the same word in the same way. It may not be valid to assume, for example, that the word "faith" is the same term in Romans as in the Epistle to the Hebrews; for in fact it seems to have a different emphasis in each of these books.[45]

Besides some of the works mentioned in connection with etymology, the following will be of assistance in the study of the usage of words in both Biblical and extra-Biblical writings: the Septuagint, which is a Greek translation of the Old Testament; the Greek Classics, such as the works of Plato;

the writings of the Apostolic and post-Apostolic periods; Moulton and Milligan, *The Vocabulary of the Greek Testament;* Wieand's harmony of the Gospels in the text of the Revised Standard Version or other harmonies either in the English or in the original, such as those by Burton and Robinson; and Young's *Analytical Concordance to the Bible* or other concordances, such as Cruden's.[46]

A further means of determining the precise meaning of a term is to compare and contrast it with those words which are *synonymous* with it. Trench's *Synonyms of the New Testament* and Girdlestone's *Synonyms of the Old Testament* are based on this approach. A comparative study of the synonymous words for "sin" in both the Old and New Testaments will afford an excellent illustration of the value of this procedure.

Included also in the discovery of the definition of Biblical terms should be a *comparative study of the various outstanding translations,* which represent the attempts of experts to convey in the vernacular the meaning of the original terminology of the Scriptures. Among these translations are the following: American Revised Version, Revised Standard Version of the New Testament, Moffatt's translation of the Old and New Testaments, Weymouth's translation of the New Testament, and the American translation of the Bible, which includes Goodspeed's translation of the New Testament. Many others of varying worth could be enumerated.[47]

The ancient versions may also be placed in the category of translations, although they are not as significant as the vernacular for the study of the English Bible. Besides the Septuagint, which was previously mentioned, Terry lists the following:

> . . . the Vulgate, the Peshito-Syriac Version, the Targums, or Chaldee Paraphrases of the Old Testament, especially that of Onkelos on the Pentateuch, and Jonathan Ben Uzziel on the Prophets, and the

Greek versions of Aquila, Symmachus, and Theodotion.

To these he adds the Arabic, Coptic, Aethiopic, Armenian, and Gothic versions, which, he indicates, ". . . are of less value, and, in determining the meaning of rare words, cannot be relied on as having any considerable weight or authority." [48]

It is sometimes helpful to employ the science of *comparative philology* in the exposition of Biblical terms. This involves the tracing of words through a family of languages. Lexicons will sometimes provide information along this line.

Another important consideration in the definition of Biblical terms concerns the significance of the *kind* of term present, that is, whether it is literal or figurative. [49] One may have observed, for example, the use of the figurative term "leaven" in Mark 8:14. On the basis of this observation, these questions may have been raised: "What is meant by 'the leaven of the Pharisees'? Why did Jesus use such an expression in this instance?"

One of the factors determining the answers to these questions involves the meaning and purpose of an image. Now the function of an image is to draw an analogy between a literal term and its spiritual counterpart in order to illuminate the spiritual truth. And it should be remembered that *in every case* such an analogy is intended to be partial, and consequently should not be forced to imply complete identicalness. Therefore, in interpreting the figurative term "leaven" one should first ascertain the spiritual qualities of the Pharisees and the characteristics of physical leaven, and then place the two side by side to determine wherein they are actually analogous. In all this one should utilize, above all, common sense and the contextual relations of a passage, for these factors are of invaluable assistance in the proper interpretation of any figurative term.

It should also be noted that at times the literal-figurative distinction cannot be made until partial interpretation has occurred. In this case, too, whether a term is literal or figurative becomes an important consideration in the expository process. Note as an example Jesus' statement in Mark 8:35-37.

Even from a reading of this brief discussion one may readily deduce that the discovery of the full meaning of all Biblical terms is an impossible task. But this fact need not lead to dismay if one is reminded that the Scriptures contain certain key words which are not too numerous. It is these words which ought to be mastered completely. To attempt to master all Biblical terms would virtually guarantee the mastery of none of them. If, however, one is selective on the basis of the selectivity of Biblical authors, then one will discover those words which are strategic and make them one's complete possession, leaving the remaining terms for less thorough study. If this procedure is followed, not only will one make the most efficient use of one's time and avoid discouragement as well, but one will also come in contact with the great ideas conveyed by the great words of the Bible.[50]

(2) Signification of Inflections [51]

Numerous examples could be given from both the Old and New Testaments to illustrate the use of inflections in the explanation of terms. However, since a multiplicity of examples in itself cannot teach one how to utilize inflections, there follows but one illustration whose main purpose is to motivate the reader to delve more deeply into the subject for himself.

Mark 11:24 reads: "Therefore I tell you, whatever you ask in prayer, believe that you receive it, and you will." The inflection of the Greek verb "receive" indicates that it is in the aorist tense. When one has observed this fact and has asked, "What is conveyed by the aorist? Why is it used in this instance?" one needs to examine the various ways in which the Greek aorist may be employed to ascertain which is utilized in this case and what its significance is. In so doing one discovers that it is sometimes used in a gnomic sense. Dana and Mantey describe this kind of aorist in the following words:

> A generally accepted fact or truth may be regarded as so fixed in its certainty or axiomatic in its character that it is described by the aorist, just as though it were an actual occurrence. For this idiom we commonly employ the general present.[52]

It is entirely possible, then, that it is the gnomic aorist which is being utilized in Mark 11:24; and if it is, then the force of the term "receive" becomes quite clear. Jesus is saying, "When you make petitions in your prayers, if you have so much faith in their answer, if you believe in their realization so strongly that for you they are as good as accomplished already, then you will certainly see their fulfilment." Jesus is suggesting that the pray-er must have such implicit faith in God that for him the petition is as good as the answer. And He assures His listeners that this kind of faith will be rewarded just as surely as was His faith in cursing the fig tree. This is but one instance of the way in which an awareness of the significance of inflections will enable the interpreter to find the deeper meaning of Scriptural terms and thereby of Scriptural statements.

Often the English translation will convey the element of inflection. Even in the preceding example, where there seems to be a contradiction between the inflection of the original and of the translation, the careful observer of the vernacular will note that the verb "receive" has the inflection of the general present rather than the future tense. One would normally expect Mark 11:24 to read thus: "Therefore I tell you, whatever you ask in prayer, believe that you *will* receive it, and you will." But, on the contrary, the auxiliary "will" indicating the future is omitted, and the present "receive" is used. On the basis of the English alone, then, one can discover that Jesus is at least hinting that the effective prayer is one in which the petitioner so strongly believes that his requests will be answered that for him what is ordinarily anticipated for the future is even now a reality. This does not seem to be as strong as the inference which may be drawn from the original if indeed the gnomic aorist is being employed by Jesus; and this serves to illustrate the fact that in the interpretation of some of the details of a passage, a knowledge of the original is indispensable for the fullest kind of exposition. Nevertheless, because much can be found in the vernacular, it may be profitably utilized by those who do not know the original; and further, it may serve as the beginning place even for the student who has a working acquaintance with the original languages.[58]

(3) Implications of Contextual Relations and Interrelations

Not only must terms be examined from the standpoint of their etymology, usage, synonyms, translations, comparative philology, kinds, and inflections, but also on the basis of the structural relations and interrelations which form a labyrinth of factors whose implications must be considered in the interpretive process. How complicated they are may be readily seen when all the various connections which were previously enumerated are placed side by side.[54] They entail relations and interrelations both immediate and remote, within phrases of clauses of sentences of paragraphs of segments of subsections of sections of divisions of books of groups of books.[55] They include all that is involved in the movement and intermovement, the action and interaction of thought. Thus it may truly be said that *the context of each term of a book is the book itself.*

The purpose of emphasizing the complexity of contextual

relations and their interpretive significance is to encourage the reader to be constantly on his guard lest he forget to utilize some important structural connections in the process of exposition. For such an oversight will eventuate either in erroneous interpretation or at least incomplete interpretation. In fact, it was because of this that the suggestion was made that an entire passage be observed before a serious attempt be made to interpret any of its parts. It might even be added that the exegesis of each unit within a given book should remain tentative until the entire book is studied in order to give full consideration to the broader structural relations, which are frequently so important for proper exposition.

By way of elucidation, there follows a brief illustration of how contextual relations are significant in the interpretation of the individual statements of Romans 12:1-15:13. The first part affords an example of the importance of the more immediate contextual relations, whereas the latter part concerns the significance of remote relations.

One notes that the connection between Romans 12:1-2 and 12:3ff. is that described heretofore as ideological particularization, which involves the movement from the general to the specific. The general statement contains several major parts: first, an exhortation to the Romans to present their bodies as a living sacrifice; second, the indication that such a sacrifice constitutes spiritual worship; third, an exhortation involving the contrast between the conformed and the transformed life; and fourth, the means and purpose of such a life, namely, through a renewed intelligence to discern God's good and acceptable and perfect will.

When one applies the law of particularization and attempts to discover wherein these general ideas are explicated by the particulars of 12:3ff., one finds that for Paul the living sacrifice of the body involves the proper evaluation of one's own gifts, avoiding conceit, loving others genuinely, hating evil, showing hospitality, blessing those who curse one, living in empathy with one's fellow Christians, etc. These are concrete expressions of the sacrificial life. As a matter of fact, these and other practices found in chapters 12:3-15:13 constitute God's good and acceptable and perfect will, which the Romans are enabled to discern if they surrender themselves to Him. These are the elements involved in the transformed life, rather than the life which is molded according to the world. The people of this world persecute those who persecute them, repay evil for evil. If the Roman Christians are like the world, they will do the same. But if through dedication to God their mental outlooks are changed, then if their enemy hungers, they will feed him; if he thirsts, they will give him to drink. They will overcome evil with good. This kind of surrender to God and His will is spiritual worship, the liturgy which engages the very heart of man. Paul is saying in effect to the Romans: "Do you want to worship with the spirit and therefore truly? Then bless those who persecute you instead of cursing them. Give your enemy food and drink. That constitutes true worship. Without it worship is ritualistic, formalistic, empty. Only the transformed life is the life of spiritual worship!" The examination of the significance and outworkings of the relation of particularization thus enables one to arrive at the deeper meaning of Paul's statements in Romans 12:1-15:13.

But there is much more to the exposition of Romans 12:1ff. than this. For one thing, note that the first verse contains a "therefore," indicating that this passage presents the effects of preceding causes, in other words, that the law of ideological causation is operative in the arrangement of the Epistle. This throws the interpreter into the more remote contextual relations of this passage. Consequently, if he is to ascertain the full impact of the exhortations of Romans 12:1-15:13, he must find in the first eleven chapters the grounds which make imperative obedience to them. This in turn involves the study of all the relations and interrelations of chapters 1-11. Such a study cannot be made at this point, but the reader can probably see some of the potentialities inherent in the exploitation of all these structural relations. It is further evident what a complexity of connections and interconnections must often be taken into consideration in the interpretation of a passage.

(4) Connotations of General Literary Forms

Some of the interpretive implications of general literary forms were indicated in their previous treatment.[56] The purpose of the discussion at this juncture is to supply one or two illustrations which will clarify some of the means by which the utilization of literary forms will have a serious bearing on exegesis, and to suggest articles and books which may be read in order to broaden the reader's understanding of their exegetical importance.

Let us consider, for example, one of the factors involved in the interpretive significance of the parabolic form. As was indicated previously, the parable is based on an analogy between a brief physical narrative and a spiritual truth. Now such an analogy does not imply that the spiritual truth and the physical illustration are absolutely identical, since spiritual and physical truth are on two different planes and can never be equated. Nor need they be, for all that is demanded of an analogy is similarity at certain points. In fact, it is safe to limit the place of intersection between the spiritual truth and the physical illustration to one main point.

If this analysis is true, one of the factors involved in the exegetical significance of the parabolic form becomes abundantly clear. The physical aspects of the parable should never be pressed in all its particulars in order to discover its meaning. For the parable may be likened to a husk containing a kernel. The husk must be removed until the kernel alone remains, because it is for the sake of the kernel that the husk exists. The kernel may be compared with the one, main spiritual truth for which the parable is given. When this kernel is discovered, the physical aspect, like the husk, may be set aside. For to treat the physical factor of the parable as identical with the spiritual truth it carries, and consequently to find spiritual meaning in every particular of the narrative, is to misuse the parabolic form.[57]

Similarly, apocalyptic literature has certain peculiar characteristics which must be utilized in its interpretation. For instance, the symbolism of apocalyptic literature is just as strict in its own way as the more literal language of the Gospels. In this connection Benjamin A. Warfield states:

> The apocalypse is written in a language of its own, having its own laws, in accordance with which it must be interpreted. There is such a thing as a grammar of apocalyptical symbolism; and what is meant by the various images is no more a matter for the imagination to settle than are points of Greek syntax.[58]

If this principle alone were utilized in the exegesis of the symbols of the Revelation, many fallacious explanations would be avoided.

Another important interpretive factor inherent in the apocalyptic form is its timelessness. It views history panoramically without giving much attention to temporal progress. Thus an apocalyptic passage will frequently refer to principles whose historical fulfilment is separated by millennia without supplying adequate indications as to the time span involved. Jesus' discourse in Mark 13 may be said to reveal this characteristic. In view of this fact, it is much sounder to explain apocalyptic literature in terms of basic, universal, spiritual principles rather than in terms of a concrete historical timetable. For to subject it to the temporal criteria which are applied to prose narrative is to insure its misunderstanding.

These are but meager illustrations of that which is involved in the interpretive implications of general literary forms. However, it is hoped that through them the reader will begin realizing the great importance of becoming thoroughly acquainted with them to the end that he may become a more efficient expositor. In order to facilitate the accomplishment of this most worthwhile objective, the reader is urged to examine some of the following books or comparable ones.

Arnot, *The Parables of Our Lord*
Baldwin, *Types of Literature in the Old Testament*
Barton, *Hebrew Poetry*
Bewer, *Literature of the Old Testament*
Bruce, *The Parabolic Teaching of Christ*
Cobb, *Criticism of Systems of Hebrew Metre*
Deane, *Pseudepigrapha*
Dodd, *The Parables of the Kingdom*
Drummond, *Jewish Messiah*
Gardiner, *The Bible as Literature*
Genung, *Guidebook to Biblical Literature*
Gordon, *The Poets of the Old Testament*
Gray, *The Forms of Hebrew Poetry*
International Standard Bible Encyclopedia, Articles on "Apocalyptic Literature," "Poetry, Hebrew," and "Poetry, New Testament"
King, *Early Religious Poetry of the Hebrews*
Lowth, *Hebrew Poetry*
McIvor, *The Literary Study of the Prophets*
Moffatt, *The Bible, a New Translation*
Moulton, *Modern Reader's Bible*
　　　The Literary Study of the Bible
Schurer, *Jewish People*
Smith, *The Early Poetry of Israel*
Stanton, *Jewish and Christian Messiah*
Trench, *Notes on the Parables of Our Lord*
Wild, *Literary Guide to the Bible*

(5) Import of Atmosphere

At times the faithful application of the factor of atmosphere is significant in determining the correct answers to interpretive questions. An example of a passage where this may be true is Romans 9-11. In fact, Paul himself devotes the opening of chapter 9 to make clear and forceful the underlying tone of the entire unit lest it be expounded apart from his controlling attitude and thereby misinterpreted. Note the emphatic way in which he states his feelings. The verses read:

I am speaking the *truth in Christ, I am not lying;* my *conscience* bears me witness in the *Holy Spirit,* that I have *great* sorrow and *unceasing* anguish in my *heart.* For I could wish that *I myself* were *accursed* and *cut off from Christ* for the sake of *my brethren, my kinsmen by race.* They are *Israelites,* and to them belong the *sonship, the glory,* the *covenants,* the giving of the *law,* the *worship,* and the *promises;* to them belong the *patriarchs,* and of their race, according to the flesh, is the *Christ.* God who is over all be blessed forever. Amen.

Apparently Paul wants it unmistakably understood that all he is about to say grows out of a grave concern and a self-sacrificial love in behalf of Israel, and an empathy which includes a profound appreciation of their unique position. He is saying, in effect, "Let nothing that I say be construed otherwise. There is nothing in my heart of hatred or bitterness or belittlement." A constant utilization of this atmospheric element will help in discovering the connotations of Paul's statements in these chapters, some of which consist of strong condemnations of Israel.

For other examples which reveal the importance of employing the factor of atmosphere in the interpretive process, see Romans 1:8-17, Philippians, and I Peter. It should be noted that atmosphere is often closely related to an author's purpose and viewpoint, which will be discussed next.[59]

(6) Author's Purpose and Viewpoint

The proper approach to any work of art in order to guarantee impartial and therefore accurate interpretation is to stand in the shoes of the author himself, to adopt his mentality and peculiar point of view. The time will eventually come when one will be able to decide for oneself whether or not an artist's point of view is valid. But such a decision must await one's sympathetic identification with the artist.

For instance, to expound validly the book of Jude, one must see it from the standpoint of Jude himself. The condemnations of the book will appear bitter and unwarranted unless the interpreter of Jude attempts to stand where Jude is standing. Likewise, the interpretation of the miracles becomes much more sound and rich when one views them from the standpoint of the Gospel writers. The determination of whether a passage is literal or figurative must also be based on a consideration of what the author had in mind when he wrote it. These are a few examples of how an awareness of the writer's standpoint enhances one's understanding of his work.

It is recognized that at times there is difficulty in discovering the purpose and point of view of an author. However, this should not deter the expositor from doing his utmost to empathize with the author's outlook before he attempts to interpret and evaluate his work.[60]

(7) Historical Background

Because the books of the Bible were written in a specific historical setting, and because they were addressed to those who lived in a concrete historical situation, it is imperative that one utilize their historical background if one is to recreate the message of their authors.

Among other things, the discovery of a book's historical

setting includes these elements: the date, place, and occasion of writing; the identity of the author and the recipients; the characteristics and problems of the readers; contemporary literature, customs, and beliefs; the social, political, geographical, and spiritual environment of author, recipients, and characters, together with their background.

It should be stressed, however, that at times it is impossible to ascertain some of these factors with absolute assurance. The primary point, therefore, is that one ought to do one's utmost to discover the historical setting of each Biblical book, and that one should use what is found in its interpretation. In other words, it is the fact of the recognition and utilization of the historical principle rather than the complete dependence of exegesis upon an exhaustive and certain knowledge of all the historical data which is of prime importance.

It is in connection with the discovery of historical background that the findings of archaeology are relevant. For through it much has been learned about the historical setting of Biblical books which otherwise would not have been known.

In order to foster in the reader an awareness of the interpretive significance of the historical background of Scriptural books, it is recommended that some of the following books be perused.

Albright, *The Archaeology of Palestine and the Bible*
Breasted, *Ancient Times*
      A History of Egypt from the Earliest Time to the Persian Conquest
Burrows, *What Mean These Stones?*
Caiger, *Bible and Spade*
Charles, *Religious Development Between the Old and New Testaments*
Cook, *The Religion of Ancient Palestine in the Light of Archaeology*

Dalman, *Sacred Sites and Ways*
Fairweather, *Background of the Gospels*
Finegan, *Light from the Ancient Past*
Glover, *The World of the New Testament*
Guignebert, *The Jewish World in the Time of Jesus*
Kittel, *A History of the Hebrews*
Macgregor, *Jew and Greek: Tutors unto Christ*
Montgomery, *The Samaritans*
Moore, *Judaism in the First Centuries of the Christian
     Era*
Nilsson, *The Historical Hellenistic Background of the
     New Testament*
Oesterley, *The Jews and Judaism During the Greek Period*
Oesterley and Robinson, *Sacrifices in Ancient Israel*
Rogers, *A History of Ancient Persia*
     A History of Babylonia and Assyria
Schurer, *A History of the Jewish People in the Time of
     Christ*
Smith, *The Historical Geography of the Holy Land*
Welch, *Post-Exilic Judaism*
Wright, *The Westminster Historical Atlas to the Bible* [61]

(8) Psychological Factor

Since human experience transcends its literary expression,
the true expositor of the Scriptures will search for more
than their linguistic phenomena. He will look for emotions,
desires, hopes, motives, thoughts, attitudes. He will make the
object of his quest the disclosure of the self-consciousness
of Biblical authors and characters. He will see beyond the
symbols to the reality, namely, the experience of which
Scriptural literature is but the product and the means of
conveyance.

An example of the application of this psychological factor
is involved in the interpreter's insistence that *all human actions and reactions be accounted for in terms of sufficient*

causation. When he studies the sayings and actions of Jesus, for instance, he will know that they presuppose a certain kind of self-consciousness. Further, he will be aware that Jesus' self-consciousness must be interpreted in such a way as to be adequate for its expressions, and that its expressions will correspond to the self-consciousness which gave them birth. He will realize that to expound Jesus' self-consciousness so as not to provide sufficient causation for its outward manifestations is to violate the principles of experience. And he will know that to violate psychological principles is to misinterpret the Scriptures.

It is good to be aware of the danger of subjectiveness in the use of the psychological factor in Biblical exegesis. It should be remembered, however, that such a danger is not indispensable to the factor itself. If care is taken in its use, it will eventuate in the realization of great insights into Scriptural truth.[62]

(9) Ideological Implications

This expository factor is closely related to the preceding one, in that both are based on the assumption that all human communication including literature has its limitations. No means of expression can convey explicitly all that resides within the mind of its author. Therefore, there is more to understanding a literary statement than meets the physical eye.

This is not only true as regards the psychological elements, but ideologically as well. Scriptural literature contains many implications which are never explicitly stated. And what is even more significant, some of its implications are more basic and important than those ideas and facts which are overtly expressed.

For example, the Scriptures assume at the very outset the self-conscious existence of God. Nowhere in Genesis 1 is there a statement to the effect that God is, and yet this fact is logically necessary for all else. Without it creation would be impossible. Thus when one examines the rational foundations of the term "create" (*bara'*), one discovers that it presupposes much more than it outwardly asserts or than is explicitly stated elsewhere in the chapter. And if one were to overlook its implications in its interpretation, one would fail to see that which is even more fundamental than what it distinctly expresses.

If the reader is anxious to test the importance of ideological implications as well as develop his ability to discover them, let him examine a passage like Genesis 13-14 or 18-19 from the standpoint of the assumptions which Abraham makes about the character of God. Let him also note the implications of the experiences recorded in those passages. When one looks at the chapters mentioned in this light, one finds that they reveal much more about Abraham's and the author's concept of God than is discovered in the explicit statements regarding His character.[63]

(10) Progress of Revelation

In the exegesis of the Scriptures, it must be realized that the Divine self-disclosure which they embody partakes of the element of progression. Not only is this true in regard to the movement from the Old Testament to the New Testament, but also in regard to the revelation found within the two Testaments.

The process of revelation found in the Scriptures is never static; rather it is dynamic. In fact, it may be said that at times it is retrogressive rather than progressive. But it is moving, and moving steadily from the lower to the higher, from the lesser to the greater, from the partial to the total, from the temporary to the final.

If this be true, one should never interpret the Old Testament as if it were the New Testament, any more than one should read last year's newspaper as if it were today's paper. Now this does not imply that the Old Testament is com-

pletely obsolete and therefore worthless. For even copies of
old newspapers are kept because they contribute much to
an understanding of that which is happening today. The
same function is performed by the Old Testament in relation to the New Testament. But this implies that the Old
Testament is preparatory and partial, whereas the New
Testament is the final fulfilment. If this be so, then it is
essential that one never interpret the incomplete as if it were
complete, the preparation as if it were the fulfilment. In
fine, the New Testament concept of God should not be read
into the Old Testament. To fail to follow this basic principle is to assure eisegesis.

These statements regarding the relation of the two Testaments are substantiated by both the Old Testament and the
New Testament themselves. They require such an approach
by their very nature and their statements. The Old Testament is *old*, and the New Testament is *new*. The Old Testament constantly looks forward; the New Testament points
backward. In fact, the whole New Testament concept of the
person of Jesus is involved in this principle. The author of
the Epistle to the Hebrews in 1:1-4 makes this fact abundantly clear. His thesis is that if Jesus is truly the Son of God,
then He is in substance the same as His Father. And the
One who is essentially identical with God is in turn the most
complete revealer of God. For He not only reveals God, but
is God revealed. If this be true, says the author of Hebrews,
then all previous revelations were embryonic and incomplete; their function was to serve as precursors of this full
and final revelation. In view of this, to place the self-disclosure of God in the Old Testament on a par with His self-
disclosure in the New Testament is in effect a denial of the
Sonship of Jesus. And to deny the Sonship of Jesus is to
deny the very essence of the New Testament, in which His
Sonship is central and determinative. Thus, though the Old
Testament and the New Testament bear witness to the same
God, they themselves insist that the testimony of the New

Testament and its Christ must be interpreted as far out-shining that of the Old Testament.

However, it should be stressed further that it is just as erroneous to read the New Testament as if it had never been preceded by the Old Testament as it is to read the Old Testament as if it were the New Testament. Preparation should not be interpreted as if it were fulfilment; but neither should fulfilment be interpreted as if there were no preparation. The contribution of the Old Testament is in-dispensable to the full understanding of the New Testa-ment. Therefore, the expositor must become acquainted with the terms, symbolism, expectations, and theology of the Old Testament if the richness of the New Testament is to become his possession. For the nature of Scriptural history itself demands it.

The element of progressive revelation within the Testa-ments must also be considered in Biblical hermeneutics. The book of Genesis, for example, should not be interpreted as if its revelation were on the same level as that of Isaiah. Although the two periods are organically related, the pro-phetic period transcends the patriarchal period in regard to God's self-disclosure.

Now there is no doubt that the application of the concept of progressive revelation has resulted in many false conclu-sions. But here, as in many other instances, the fault lies not in the principle but in its application or, rather, its mis-application. To misemploy it is unquestionably dangerous; to overlook it is equally dangerous. *For the standpoint of the Scriptures themselves must be taken into account in their exegesis. And the standpoint to which they constantly bear witness is that God has progressively revealed Himself to men.*[64]

(11) Organic Unity

The essential harmony of the books of the Bible was one of the determinative principles in the formation of the

canon. And the more one studies them, the more one becomes convinced of the reality of their fundamental oneness.

If this conviction is sound, then it is valid to use Scripture
to expound Scripture. In so doing one should take great
care to avoid two dangers: first, the relating of unlike and
disconnected passages; and second, the disregarding of the
factor of progressive revelation. If, on the other hand, comparable materials are used, especially from the standpoint
of historical placement, this factor can be very beneficial in
gaining insight into Scriptural passages.

The principle of organic unity is also helpful as a corrective to misinterpretation. For if parts of the Scriptures which
should be in agreement, such as the Gospels, are expounded
so as to make them appear contradictory, then one has a
right to question the soundness of one's interpretation. And
one will usually find that if the data are seriously and sin-
cerely re-examined, the apparent contradictions will dis-
appear.

In fact, in view of the fundamental oneness of the Scriptures, it can safely be said that there are no substantial contradictions within them, no matter which passages are compared. There may be differences, some of which will be
noted later.[65] But these are not of an essential nature. This
fact is of great consequence in the guidance of Biblical
interpretation.

(12) Inductive View of Inspiration

Sound Biblical exegesis is not possible apart from proper
allowance for the dual nature of the Scriptures. For they
themselves attest the fact that they consist of Divine revelation realized through human instrumentation. It should be
remembered, therefore, that the Divine inspiration which
accounts for the experience which produced the Scriptures
did not occur in a vacuum. God operated through human
agents who had certain mental abilities and certain other

talents, whose religious experience was of a certain quality, who lived in a certain environment which involved certain geographical, social, political, economic, and religious factors, and who had a certain heritage. And these specific historical factors inevitably had their influence on the writing of Biblical literature.

In fact, it may legitimately be said that God Himself is limited by the individual qualities and abilities and the specific age of the persons to whom He discloses Himself and through whom He chooses to work. This is true because God has so ordained it by the very nature which He gave to men. And because God will not negate that which He originally ordained, He does not nullify the singular individuality of those whom He inspires.

Proper allowance for the human aspect of Scriptural inspiration clarifies the reason for many of the interpretive factors heretofore mentioned. For example, it accounts for differing literary forms. Paul could never have written the Psalms, and David could never have written the Epistle to the Romans. Individual differences in talent and age are the causes for the use of particular terminology and the employment of certain symbols, expressions, and practices. The need for considering the progressive nature of revelation is also due to this factor. The development of God's self-disclosure to man is not caused by God's intellectual and spiritual growth. It is rather necessitated by human limitations which God Himself does not disregard. Men were not ready to receive God's full revelation until they had been prepared for it.[66] This is not to say that men cannot be changed; but even in doing that which will result in their transformation, God is limited by certain human traits and circumstances. It is therefore imperative that one's view of inspiration make adequate allowance for both the Divine and human nature of the Scriptures. For the very character of the Scriptures themselves demands it.

(13) Textual Criticism

Because we do not possess any of the original Scriptural documents, it sometimes becomes necessary to employ textual or lower criticism in order to ascertain the true reading of the text. Three basic steps are followed in this process. First, the manuscript evidence is collected, investigated, and evaluated. In its evaluation there is a tendency to assign the greatest weight to older manuscripts. Second, when the evidence from the manuscripts is not decisive, the reading which best fits into the context is chosen. And third, if neither manuscript evidence nor the contextual factor is decisive, then the unusual reading is favored. This is done because there would be little occasion to alter the text so as to make possible an unusual reading, whereas it is understandable how a copyist might change it for the purpose of clarification or to make it harmonize with the seeming demands of reason.[67]

The following are some books which may be examined in order to become better acquainted with this factor.

Buhl, *Canon and Text of the Old Testament*
Green, *General Introduction to the Old Testament: The Text*
Kenyon, *Recent Developments in the Textual Criticism of the Greek Bible*
The Text of the Greek Bible
Nestle, *Introduction to the Textual Criticism of the Greek New Testament*
Robertson, *An Introduction to the Textual Criticism of the New Testament*
Studies in the Text of the New Testament
Scrivener, *A Plain Introduction to the Criticism of the New Testament*
Vincent, *History of Textual Criticism*

(14) Interpretations of Others

An investigation of the views of others serves two purposes: first, it confronts one with certain interpretive factors which may have been overlooked or misapplied; and second, it reveals the exegetical conclusions which others, many of whom are experts, have made when they have utilized the available data. Both of these functions are important, but it is the latter which is of primary interest at this point.

In connection with this aspect, Dana makes these significant statements:

> Interpretation is a social process. The best results can be achieved only by the cooperation of many minds. The results of the scholars in one age are the natural and rightful heritage of those who labor in the same field in succeeding ages, and should be used by them. No interpreter of the New Testament can wisely ignore the results wrought by past generations and strike out for totally independent and original conclusions on all points. He should become familiar as far as possible with what has previously been accomplished . . . The commentaries which have been produced by the scholarship of the past form a very essential part of the materials for interpretation.[68]

The importance of examining the historical exegetical views on a given passage should be especially stressed. That is, not only should modern or near modern commentators be read, but one ought to attempt to discover the interpretations held by outstanding men throughout the history of the Christian Church. This is particularly necessary when one is studying a difficult portion which is susceptible of various explanations.

The reader will note the relative place of this exegetical factor in this list. In the minds of many, the first step in

Bible study as-a-whole as well as in the interpretive process is to consult secondary sources. This manual has suggested that in both methodical study in general and the exegetical phase in particular the firsthand study of the Scriptures should be primary in order and in rank.

Some of the major reasons for this emphasis have already been stated.[69] It only remains to clarify what it involves in connection with exposition. It does not imply that the examination of the text itself in terms of the observational and interpretive practices heretofore suggested should be completely exhausted before one resorts to commentaries. Rather it stresses the fact that independent study ought to be the initial step. When a reasonable amount of time has been devoted to it, then the interpreter should investigate secondary sources. And after there has been a partial investigation of secondary sources, there should be a return to firsthand observation and interpretation. Then there may follow a further examination of exegetical opinion. The interpreter thus becomes engaged in a recurring cycle which need never cease, especially from the standpoint of firsthand investigation. Thus firsthand study serves as the initial step of observation and interpretation as well as that to which one constantly returns. The consequence of this approach will be a freshness and enthusiasm and fruitfulness in Bible study which cannot otherwise be attained.[70]

To summarize, this is the principle which is the foundation of all true hermeneutics: *the interpretation of Scriptures must reflect the nature and requirements of the Scriptures themselves. Their properties and outlook should dictate what factors are to be used in their exegesis.* For example, because they deal with spiritual matters, they require spiritual sensitivity for their interpretation. Because the Bible is a library of books, each of which is written by a certain person in a certain historical situation using certain terminology and certain literary forms, it follows that these and related considerations must be utilized in the exegetical process. If this basic hermeneutical principle is made the ground of all Biblical exposition, there will follow the kind of interpretation which befits the Scriptures.

Several facts should be noted regarding these determinants of interpretation.

First, they are all interrelated, some more than others. In spite of this fact, an effort was made to distinguish between them because of the values of such an analysis in making one conscious of the various factors which influence interpretation.

Second, this discussion of exegetical determinants is of necessity merely suggestive. Besides the books indicated in connection with individual factors, the reader is urged to study one or more of the following books on hermeneutics.

Dana, *Searching the Scriptures*
Davidson, *Sacred Hermeneutics*
Fairbairn, *Hermeneutical Manual*
Lund, *Hermeneutics*
Terry, *Biblical Hermeneutics*

Third, the factors described as objective may be classified further as to whether they are internal or external in relation to the text. Contextual relations, for example, are internal, whereas historical background contains external elements.

Fourth, these ingredients of exposition are of varying importance, depending somewhat on the particular passage being interpreted. Furthermore, the nature of the unit being studied as well as the nature of the ingredients determine which of them must be consciously brought to bear, which are applied implicitly, and which are irrelevant.

Fifth, the listing of these determinants does not imply a rigid formula for interpretation. It is not expected that one will consider each of them in turn every time one wants to interpret a term. Rather their purpose is to enable the reader to develop *interpretive instincts*. True, he may find it necessary consciously to apply these factors one by one for a time, just as one learning to drive an automobile must consciously follow the steps involved in driving. But the ultimate purpose for so doing is that interpretation like driving may become a matter of second nature.[71]

Sixth, one must use discretion in the application of these determinants. The reader should not infer that in the study of every portion of Scripture all of them must be exhausted before one can proceed to the next phase of study. One must be selective both in the choice of the interpretive questions to be answered and in the use of those factors which govern their answers.

Seventh, because of the lack of space some of these determinants were stated without an adequate presentation of the particulars on which they were based. It is not expected that these will be accepted without an inductive study by the reader. This material merely represents the results of the writer's inductive study in relation to those factors which must eventually be considered in the thorough exposition of any and all passages.[72]

2. Formulation of Interpretive Answers

Several weaknesses frequently appear in the interpretive process. One of these is the fact that the expositor is often *haphazard* and *disorganized* in his task because he has developed no methodical approach which he may utilize as he interprets a passage. A further weakness is a *lack of awareness* of the exegetical factors which are being employed. He is not conscious of exactly what he is doing, why he is doing it, or what he should be doing because he has not analyzed carefully the ingredients which constitute interpretation. Related to both of these is the *lack of thoroughness* in exposition. Because one applies those factors which happen to occur to him at the moment, or because one is not self-conscious in the process of exposition, one frequently forgets to utilize certain determinants which might substantially alter one's interpretation.

It is these and connected weaknesses which the reader is urged to guard against in formulating answers to interpretive questions. It is suggested that the preceding analysis of the ingredients of exposition be used as a foundation for developing a *methodical, self-conscious, thorough* approach to exegesis to the end that it may indeed accomplish its objective.

C. Interpretive Integration and Summarization

After the important interpretive questions raised in connection with a particular unit are answered, there remains the problem of integrating the various answers so as to arrive at the main message of the passage. Sometimes this is at least partially accomplished in the replies to the questions of exposition, since some of them may be integrative in nature. In any case it ought to be clear that at some stage integration must occur, and further, that such an integration should be expressed in summary form.

There are various techniques which may be employed to integrate and summarize the exegesis of a passage, some of which will now be presented.

1. It is sometimes helpful to *list the main truths* which have been found in a unit of Scripture. In so doing it may be well to attempt to distinguish between the outstanding truth or truths and those which are subordinate.

2. One may state the major theme of a passage by the use of a *descriptive title* or *proposition*. For example, the interpretation of Isaiah 5 may be summarized by the title, "God's Best and Israel's Worst." Or the primary idea of Joshua may be stated in this proposition: "The Conquest of Canaan Was Accomplished by Joshua's and Israel's Dependence upon the Indispensable and Dependable Yahweh."

3. If one is dealing with a segment, especially in narrative literature, it may be beneficial to utilize *analytical or interpretive paragraph titles.*[78]

4. The employment of an *outline* is frequently of assistance in integrating and summarizing a passage of Scripture. The outline used may be either *topical* or *logical,* depending on the nature of the passage. Generally speaking, a topical outline should not be utilized in the summarization of logical passages such as those found in the Pauline Epistles; for a topical outline cannot do justice to logical movement. The means used in summarization should be suited to the nature of the unit being considered.[74]

5. The *paraphrase* may profitably be used in this capacity.[75]

6. The *chart* is also a helpful means of integration and summarization.[76]

7. One may use the *essay form* in this connection. One or several paragraphs may be written on a unit. There are certain basic integrative questions which may be used as guides. The following are two of them: "How does the structure of the passage reveal its main purpose and message? What are the major contributions of a passage to the larger structural unit of which it is a part?"

IV. SOME ERRONEOUS KINDS OF INTERPRETATION

In order to elucidate further what is involved in accurate exposition, an attempt will be made to enumerate and discuss briefly some of the fallacious interpretive approaches which have been employed in the history of the Christian Church. It should be noted that each of these contains some truth or is motivated by at least a partially legitimate cause. An effort will be made to indicate wherein this is true. The fact that these practices involve certain elements of truth serves to make one aware that fallacious exposition is frequently the result of an extreme overemphasis on a valid but not all-inclusive phase of exegesis.[77]

A. Fragmentary Interpretation

The fragmentary interpreter treats the Scriptures as if they are merely a collection of isolated verses, each of which may be understood apart from its immediate and broad context. Such a practice is partly due to the rather arbitrary division of the Bible into chapters and verses. Furthermore, there arise occasions when it is not possible to quote long passages, and it is much simpler and convenient to utilize a verse or two. This sometimes leads to the neglect of the contextual setting of Biblical statements.

The fact is that Christian ministers are among the worst offenders in this connection. They frequently take a Scriptural expression as a text and then completely disregard its setting in their ensuing use of it. And if Christian ministers are guilty of such a practice, what can be expected of their parishioners, who depend upon them for guidance in Biblical interpretation?[78]

B. Dogmatic Interpretation

This kind of exposition has as its purpose finding support in the Scriptures for certain dogmas which have already been accepted. As a result, the Bible is explained in such a way as to substantiate certain beliefs, and all possible interpretations which may negate those beliefs are promptly and arbitrarily rejected. Such an approach is often related to fragmentary exposition in that it employs prooftexts which are torn from their contexts in order to support certain dogmas. Both the fragmentary and dogmatic approaches illustrate the fact that the Scriptures can be used to prove anything.

Both of these erroneous kinds of interpretation, however, have an element of truth in them. For they accept the prin-

ciple that the Bible should be appealed to as the authority
for that which the Christian believes. However, they fail to
examine carefully the true meaning of the authority of
Scriptures. *For the Scriptures are really authoritative only
if they are used as the basis for formulating one's beliefs,
and not if they are merely employed to support one's dogmatic positions.* The first approach begins with the Scriptures and moves to beliefs; the second begins with beliefs
and moves to the Scriptures. In the first case the Bible is
the actual authority; in the second instance the individual
is the actual authority. The former approach is objective
and valid; the latter is subjective and invalid. In brief, the
first is doctrinal, for it seeks in the Scriptures the beliefs it
contains; the second is dogmatic, for it involves the assertion
of tenets for which substantiation is to be found in the
Bible.[79]

C. Rationalistic Interpretation

The rationalist attempts to expound the Scriptures in such
a way as to make them understandable and acceptable to
the reason. Lloyd Douglas's explanation of the feeding of
the five thousand in *The Robe* is an example of this type
of approach.

There are various causes for such an emphasis. The in-
ability to believe certain Biblical facts such as miracles often
results in rationalistic interpretation. However, it sometimes
represents a rebellion against the nonrational or even irrational credulity which many exercise in relation to the Scriptures. Rationalism reminds us that exegesis must involve the
use of reason, and that there should be a sincere attempt to
comprehend the message of the Bible. However, the rationalist needs to be made aware that man's reason is finite, and
that the Scriptures can therefore never be emptied of their
mystery. Man is more than reason, and he must approach the
Scriptures with all that he is.[80]

D. Mythological Interpretation

The mythological approach is closely related to the preceding type in that it is often an expression of rationalism. For frequently in order to remove that which cannot be comprehended or accepted by the reason, one will declare that certain events are myths rather than actual historical occurrences. They are therefore like the shell of a walnut which may be discarded as soon as the spiritual truth it conveys, which is the nutmeat, is discovered.

Such an approach serves to remove to a great extent the historical aspect of Scriptures by insisting that there is no indispensable relation between history and the conveyance of spiritual truth. This will often result in the position that the Gospels contain the Christ-myth. The resurrection, it is held by some who utilize this approach, was not a real historical event. It was a myth whose purpose it was to teach the supreme spiritual truth that though Jesus was slain, His spirit still lives. And when one learns this important spiritual lesson, he may then discard the "story" which was used to express it.

Now it is evident that such an approach utilizes a very significant principle of interpretation and evaluation, namely, that the spiritual truths communicated by the narratives of the Scriptures are more important than the narratives themselves, and that the narratives are therefore the means to an end. However, although it is true that the spiritual lesson is the end and therefore more important than the means, *it does not follow that the means are of no importance at all.* There is a difference between the more important and less important on the one hand, and the more important and the unimportant on the other. To express it in other words, it is often true that means are inseparably and inherently related to their ends. Therefore, to use the image of the shell and the nutmeat is sometimes erroneous. In certain instances it is more valid to use the image of the apple.

For although the peeling of an apple forms its protective covering, it cannot be removed without affecting the essence and value of the apple. Or the image of a building may legitimately be employed. The foundation of a building is the means of enabling the building to stand, for which purpose the foundation was built. However, when the building has been erected, the foundation cannot then be removed without destroying the building as well.

To illustrate further, suppose a certain man, whom we shall call Mr. A, goes to the home of a friend, Mr. B, and tells him how he has made a substantial donation to the Church at a great sacrifice. On the basis of this personal example, he pleads with Mr. B to do likewise in order to help the Church fulfil its solemn obligations. Mr. B, being moved by the example and pleading of Mr. A, decides that he too should give to the Church even if it means real self-denial. But after some investigation he discovers that Mr. A was telling him a "story" or a "myth" regarding his own self-sacrificial giving. Mr. A had not actually made a donation at all, but had concocted a story in order to teach Mr. B the important spiritual lesson of the self-sacrificial life. Having discovered this fact, what would Mr. B's reaction be? Would Mr. A's plea have the same moral force as it had when he assumed that Mr. A was relating an actual historical occurrence? Was Mr. A's story a mere means which could be discarded without affecting the end? Or was it inseparably connected with the spiritual truth it conveyed? The answers are obvious! The personal experience was indispensable to its spiritual lesson. Thus, though one may sometimes teach the content of certain truths by the use of myths, as did Plato, it takes historical occurrences to supply the kind of motivation needed in order to accept and obey such truths. If myths can afford such a motivation, it is only because they reflect what actually happens in human experience.

E. Historical Interpretation

The opposite view from the one just described is the purely historical approach to the Scriptures. There are those to whom the study of the Scriptures is primarily the study of the history of certain peoples. Such an approach fails to realize that the Scriptures contain more than history; they involve history with spiritual implications and with a spiritual purpose. The history is the means to an end. One cannot therefore limit the process of exegesis to an examination of the means. One must also become aware of the objective if one is to discover the full meaning of the Scriptures.

The historical view, however, reminds us of the important truth that the Biblical message has an historical foundation. How truly important it is was demonstrated in the discussion of mythological interpretation. However, as important as the historical foundation may be, it is still the foundation. And a foundation exists for the sake of the building.[81]

F. Allegorical Interpretation

The allegorical view is often used, for example, in the explanation of the parables. Instead of expounding them as parables, that is, as extended similes, those who use this approach interpret them as allegories or extended metaphors. Consequently, every detail is pressed for spiritual meaning.[82]

However, a more significant and dangerous form of allegorical explanation concerns the treatment of historical narratives. Those who utilize the allegorical approach frequently accept such narratives as historical, but instead of expounding their meaning in view of their concrete historical setting, they use them as allegories to teach spiritual lessons. And although the lessons drawn from them frequently are true because they are based on a general awareness of the Biblical message, they have no organic relation to the historical narratives being explained. Such an approach, to say the least, is very enticing, but it is also deceptive. For often the crossing of the line of demarcation between grammatico-historical and allegorical exposition is almost imperceptible. Therefore, the person who is concerned about valid exegesis should beware of this kind of exposition.

In order to understand the reasons for the allegorical view, one must be aware of its philosophical basis, which is that the purpose of the physical is to convey spiritual truths. The universe is one grand sacrament. For example, there is no accidental relation between the way in which the seed grows and the development of the kingdom of God. Jesus used the image of the seed to describe the nature of the Word because He was able to discern God's sacramental purpose in causing the physical seed to develop as it does. Further, the reason why God designed physical generation so as to make it dependent upon fatherhood was to teach men His own character and His relation to them. When therefore Jesus used the image of the father, He was not simply suggesting an accidental similarity between human fathers and the Divine Father. He was rather implying that the relation between the physical image and the spiritual conception was purposeful and essential.

Many of us would probably agree to some extent with this philosophy of life. However, we would not thereby justify the use of the allegorical view in explaining any and all parts of the Scripture. For in the first place, it takes unusual insight to explain correctly the spiritual meaning of the physical world. But more important, the fact is that the expounder of the Bible should not be primarily interested in interpreting life in general, but rather in explaining validly specific Biblical passages.

If this is true, then the basic question which should concern the interpreter is this: "What means was the author utilizing and what was his purpose in recording these events?" Now an author may use one of two ways of conveying spiritual lessons. He may employ the historical approach, which is direct, or the parabolic or allegorical approach, which is indirect. And the primary problem of the expositor is to discover which of these the writer was employing and to interpret the passage accordingly. If he was utilizing the direct method, then valid exposition must be limited to the direct method. If he was utilizing the indirect approach, then the expositor should also utilize the indirect approach.

Now it is evident that Jesus in His parables employed the indirect method. True, His parables reflected actual experiences, but He was not describing a concrete historical event like the crucifixion. It is therefore valid to explain Jesus' parables on the basis of the indirect means of conveying spiritual truth. However, to explain the crucifixion in the same manner would be to miss its primary meaning. The crucifixion was not meant to be a parable; its method of communicating truth is direct. To summarize, there is an essential difference between the parabolic and allegorical method of conveying truth on the one hand, and the historical method on the other. And the interpreter must discover which a writer is using and expound the passage accordingly if he is to ascertain its intended meaning.[33]

In order further to clarify the preceding remarks, the following distinction should be made. There is a vital difference between true conclusions and accurate or valid conclusions in relation to interpretation. The lessons one draws from a passage may be true, that is, in general keeping with Scriptural facts and with reality, simply because one is sufficiently acquainted with the Bible to be able to draw conclusions which are congruous with it. However, this does not imply that one's conclusions represent a valid exegesis of the passage. For valid conclusions are those which legitimately grow out of a particular passage, and not merely those which generally correspond with Biblical truth. Thus though the allegorical interpreter may draw lessons from a unit which are true, they are not necessarily accurate. And what the expositor should strive for are *accurate* deductions.

G. Literal Interpretation

Those who utilize this type of interpretation insist that the Scriptures, by and large, must be explained literally. Of course, it is impossible to be a thoroughgoing literalist, for one is coerced to interpret some statements figuratively. On the other hand, the literalist will explain many figurative passages in the literal sense because of his fear of diluting Scriptural truth.

This approach reminds us that there are some passages that must be interpreted literally. Biblical authors often employ literal statements to convey their ideas. And where they use the literal means to express their thoughts, the expositor must employ the corresponding means to explain those thoughts, namely, the literal approach. On the other hand, it is equally true that Biblical writers frequently utilize the figurative method of communicating truth; and in those cases the expositor must likewise use the figurative approach if he is to understand their message. And the literalist who forgets this fact in his zeal for safeguarding the truth of the Scriptures negates the very thing he is attempting so jealously to protect.

One of the main reasons for the error of the literalist is that he tends to equate the literal with the historical and the figurative with the unhistorical. He thus perpetrates a logical offense, for he inseparably relates the historical fact and its literary expression. He fails to realize that literal and figurative approaches are not necessarily concerned respectively with fact and fiction. For they are simply two forms of literary expression; and an event which has actually occurred may be communicated by an author by either means. Consequently, the use of imagery to describe an event does not inevitably negate its historicity.

Thus one may hold, for example, that Genesis 3 is figurative rather than literal and not necessarily imply thereby that it is substantially unhistorical rather than historical, or fictional rather than factual. The former decision involves literary interpretation; the latter concerns historical judgment. These two phases of exposition must be carefully distinguished.[84]

H. Typological Interpretation

Those who practice this approach expound the Old Testament as if at every point it foreshadows the New Testament. Even the minutest details in historical narratives are often interpreted as types which are fulfilled in the New Testament.

Such a view begins with the legitimate principle that the Old Testament is a preparation for the revelation of the New Testament, and that an important aspect of this preparation involved the use of certain symbolic practices whose purpose it was to equip Israel to understand the coming and meaning of Christ. The sacrificial system of Leviticus affords an excellent example of these.

However, it does not follow that every detail of the Old Testament is a type of the New Testament. So to understand the Old Testament is to violate two basic principles of exposition: first, that of explaining passages in view of their historical setting; and second, the principle of expounding them in the light of the author's intentions. One should be careful, therefore, not to explain accidental resemblances between occurrences in the Old and New Testaments typologically. The best policy to follow in order to avoid this danger is to limit the exposition of Old Testament symbols to those which are explained within the Scriptures themselves.

However, there is a point at which it is valid to compare the two Testaments. One frequently finds similarities between the spiritual principles of the Old Testament and those of the New Testament. When this happens, it is certainly sound to note them. However, this is far different from the practice of those who explain minor historical details as foreshadowings of the New Testament and even at times imply that they were used purposely by the author or inspired by God.

I. Predictive Interpretation

Those who follow this approach assume that the Bible is replete with predictions of future events. They therefore attempt to show how every major event which occurs was prognosticated by Scriptural writers, and in so doing they are guilty of distorting the Scriptures.

This fallacy is usually based on the failure to differentiate between prophecy and pure prediction. In prophecy the aspect of foretelling is inevitably connected with the aspect of forthtelling; in fact, its primary purpose is to support the prophet's message. Therefore, the prophet's foretelling is relevant to the concrete historical situation in which and for which he spoke. Pure prediction, on the other hand, may be totally unrelated to the historical setting in which it is made. The Scriptures contain prophecies but not pure predictions; and when one overlooks this fact, one disregards the importance of the historical element in the Scriptures and thereby misinterprets them.

The predictive approach to the Scriptures is further caused by a failure to distinguish between the various ways in which the New Testament utilizes the Old Testament. These may be divided into three classes. First, New Testament writers sometimes utilize an Old Testament prophecy whose sole fulfilment they consider to occur in New Testament times. Second, the New Testament employs Old

Testament references whose ultimate fulfilment is claimed to take place in the New Testament, but which had an immediate fulfilment in Old Testament times. The Old Testament quotation found in Matthew 1:23 probably falls into this category. This does not imply that the prophet had a double sense in mind when he spoke, but that, looking backward, the New Testament writer sees in the Old Testament statement a type which is realized in its fullest sense in the New Testament. The third use involves the comparison of New Testament statements or events with that which is found in the Old Testament. The Old Testament seems to be used in this way in Matthew 13:14-15. Jesus is saying, in effect, "The condition of the scribes and Pharisees is a supreme example and therefore a fulfilment of what Isaiah meant when he said, 'You shall indeed hear, but not understand.' " [85]

It will undoubtedly be difficult at times to determine which of the preceding uses is found in a particular New Testament passage. Nevertheless, one should be aware of them and attempt to utilize them if one is to abstain from purely predictive interpretation.

J. Systematized Interpretation

The Scriptures are often treated as if they present a systematized theology. Consequently, if, for example, a New Testament writer suggested a certain action for those to whom he was writing, that action is interpreted as an indispensable ingredient for all Christian experience. An exhortation is thus universalized on the assumption that the Scriptures contain a systematized presentation of the constituents of the spiritual life rather than statements made in particular historical situations, situations which were at times far from normal and should not be emulated.

To be more specific, because the author of Hebrews exhorted his readers to move on to maturity and to leave the alphabet of Christian principles on which they had dwelt too long (Hebrews 5:11-6:12), it is often supposed that every Christian will inevitably need that advice in his experience. It is forgotten, however, that such a view condemns everyone to duplicate the sins of New Testament churches in order to be eligible for the exhortations which were given to them. But certainly this cannot be the intent of the New Testament. Rather it should be understood that New Testament writers were addressing themselves to particular historical situations, and that their warnings were appropriate to those situations. Therefore, if any churches or individuals are guilty of the same or similar shortcomings, the exhortations are to be interpreted as being relevant to them. However, one's goal should be the avoidance of the errors of New Testament churches and a consequent avoidance of the necessity to be reproved for those errors. This represents the truest fulfilment of the purpose of the New Testament.[86]

True, one of the reasons for the systematic approach to interpretation is the legitimate need to correlate Biblical ideas and to expound the Scriptures in such a manner as to provide a pattern for the Christian life. However, in the process of satisfying this need one should not forget that the books of the New Testament were originally addressed to specific circumstances in which were found specific problems and not to an abstract universal situation. Moreover, one should not commit the grave psychological error of assuming, in effect, that everyone's experience may be coerced into precisely the same pattern.[87]

K.   Cross-Reference Interpretation

There are some who conceive of the Scriptures as a maze of cross references. As a result, they are constantly searching for similar passages, and they explain each passage in the light of comparable ones. In so doing, they often fail to take

the time to examine each unit to discover its singular meaning, and they therefore frequently make erroneous associations. The result is much faulty interpretation.

These statements do not imply that it is invalid per se to
use cross references or to associate passages. For such a procedure is involved, for example, in an examination of the
comparative usage of terms.[88] The danger to which attention is being called is the failure to interpret each unit in
its own right before blending various units together. If each
passage is first expounded as a literary entity, then valid
associations will be made, and such associations will be
beneficial. But if there occurs an amalgamation of material
before each unit is expounded in view of its own context,
then errors in exposition will be the inevitable result.

L.   Encyclopedic Interpretation

The encyclopedic interpreter treats the Bible as if it were
exhaustive, as if it contained an answer to every possible
question which might be raised. Therefore, if an answer to
a particular question is not readily found through proper
exegesis, he reads it into a passage in order that it may have
Scriptural grounds. This he insists on doing even if in
the process he reduces to absurdity certain parts of the
Scriptures.

Now it is true that the Bible contains the answers to many
of life's problems, and that it should be explained in such a
way as to provide the answers for those problems. However,
it should be remembered that the Bible is not an *Encyclo-
paedia Britannica* in the field of religion. Its historical
purpose is not to cover every possible problem which may
arise. It contains some specific answers and many general
principles. Where specific answers are found, they should be
applied; when they are lacking, the general principles
should be expounded and employed. But there should be
no attempt to read into the Scriptures specific answers to
problems which are not actually contained therein.

M. Literary Interpretation

Many of those who purportedly examine the Scriptures from the standpoint of *great* literature fail to take into account the fact that purpose is essential to greatness in literature. For they search the Bible merely for its euphonious phrases and picturesque images as if it were a purposeless collection of appealing expressions and no more.

How much more valid it is to proceed on the basis that the Bible consists of great literature not only because its literary form is worthy of praise, but also because it has a great purpose. This approach recognizes the fact that though literary form is important, it is a means to an end, and that literature must be studied on the basis of both means and end.[89]

If the reader is able to recognize these and similar erroneous kinds of interpretation when confronted by them, and if he makes a diligent effort to avoid their fallacies while at the same time carefully utilizing valid exegetical procedures, he will inevitably become a more accurate and profound interpreter of the Scriptures.[90]

V. MISCELLANEOUS SUGGESTIONS FOR INTERPRETATION

A. There are three dangers which should be avoided in exposition: *misinterpretation*, which involves ascribing the wrong meaning to a passage; *subinterpretation*, which entails the failure to ascertain the full meaning of a passage; and *superinterpretation*, which is accurate to a certain point but becomes erroneous in attributing more significance to a passage than is actually implicit in it.

B. The basic approach to the exposition of the Scriptures should be the *grammatico-historical* approach. Terry defines it to be "such an interpretation of his [the writer's] language as is required by the laws of grammar and the facts of history." [91]

C.   Because each book of the Scriptures is addressed to a concrete historical situation, its exposition should be such as to be relevant to that situation. For it is safe to assume that Biblical authors were intelligent enough to write that which was pertinent to the circumstances in which and for which they were writing. This does not imply that their literature will mean no more to us than it meant to its original readers, but that its signification to us must be organically related to its signification for them, and further, that its meaning for the present day should be distinguished from its original intent. The beginning point of exegesis should be the meaning of a Scriptural unit in its specific historical situation. If, for instance, the book of the Revelation were so interpreted, its true message would be discovered. [92]

D.   The interpreter should always keep before him the distinction between assigning meaning to the words of Scripture and discovering the meaning of the words of Scripture. The first approach is subjective and deductive; the second is objective and inductive.

E.   The easiest explanation, that is, the one which grows out of all the facts most naturally and without coercion, is usually the most accurate explanation. It is not true that the trickiest interpretation or the most mysterious one is the soundest.

F.   In a given context every Biblical term and statement has one meaning and one meaning only. Therefore, one should beware of ascribing double meanings to them.

G.   The expositor should be careful not to interpret a passage on the basis of preconceived ideas as to what it should contain. For example, he should not approach a unit with certain prejudices as to the kind of God it portrays and consequently attempt to force his theological preconceptions upon it. There is no question that such a practice is frequently followed, especially in relation to the Old Testament.[93]

H. The objective interpreter does not prejudge a passage on the basis of a traditional or denominational interpretation. He will evaluate the pros and cons of the various positions and he will choose that explanation which has in its favor the weightiest evidence. Furthermore, if the data are inconclusive, he will be honest enough to say, "I do not know for certain the meaning of this passage." Not only will such a policy eventuate in more impartial and therefore more accurate interpretations, but it will also result in a sympathetic understanding of the positions of others, as well as an understanding of the reasons for one's own position.

I. One should be constantly on the lookout for an author's interpretation of his own book, such as is found in Luke 1:1-4 or in John 20:30-31. For to ignore such statements is comparable to interpreting a map or a graph without utilizing the legend supplied by its author, or opening a lock without using the key which was made for it.

J. The principle of consistency should characterize the process of interpretation. The interpreter should be self-consistent in his exegesis and exegetical practices. Further, he should assume that an author is self-consistent in that which he writes.

K. Problems which will inevitably arise in Bible study should not be allowed to hinder the explanation of that which is abundantly clear. This does not imply that problems are insignificant and should therefore be ignored, but rather that there is the danger of becoming so problem-conscious and of developing such a problem-complex that all one sees in the Scrip-

tures is a myriad of enigmas. If this takes place, then
Biblical exegesis will be stunted before it begins.⁹⁴

L. One must often read between the lines if one is to
derive the full significance of a unit of Biblical literature. This is especially true of one's study of New
Testament epistles. For because of the very nature of
an epistle, there arises the necessity of not only attempting to discover the unstated implications of the
author, but also the readers' thoughts which are
assumed by the author. For example, Paul antici-
pates many reactions on the part of his Roman readers on the basis of his knowledge of them. And yet
he does not often state them in so many words, because there is no need to do so. Letters always assume
and imply much more than they explicitly express.
And because this is true, the expositor must make
an effort to re-create the situation in which they were
written. Such re-creation, however, needs to be
guided by the objective data of the letter itself and
by the historical facts which formed its background.
What is true of the interpretation of epistles is
basically valid in regard to other books.⁹⁵

M. The expositor should look for underlying principles
as well as specific truths in the exegesis of Biblical
passages.

N. Certain books and parts of books should be studied
together. For instance, Hosea and Amos should be
associated in interpretation, as should Job, the Wisdom Psalms, Proverbs, and Ecclesiastes. In fact, it
sometimes becomes necessary to relate certain Biblical books to extra-Biblical writings. An example of
this is the fact that Ecclesiasticus and the Wisdom of
Solomon should be studied in connection with the
Wisdom books just enumerated.

O. When interpreting a New Testament unit containing an Old Testament reference, the reference should

be studied in its original context. For it is valid to assume that New Testament writers were aware of the context of their references and ultilized them in their thinking and writing.

P.   When there are parallel passages in the Scriptures such as those which occur in the Synoptics, they should be compared. However, it should be remembered that each account is a literary entity and that therefore there should be no attempt to amalgamate the parallel units in such a way as to disregard their individuality. Their comparative study is to be supplementary to the examination of each in the light of its own contextual setting and the purpose of its particular writer.[96]

Q.   Try to develop that which characterizes the writings of C. S. Lewis, who has been described as one having a talent for putting old-fashioned truths into modern idiom.[97]

R.   It is often necessary to make very careful logical distinctions if exegetical errors are to be avoided. Some of these have already been indicated, such as the distinction between true and accurate conclusions, and between the more important and the less important on the one hand, and the more important and the unimportant on the other hand.[98] Other similar differentiations need to be made.

For example, the proper exposition of the miracles demands that one differentiate between *providential* miracles and *absolute* miracles. Providential miracles are those whose miraculous qualities are involved in their timing and in the fact that they are the fulfilment of prearranged plans and promises. The plagues and the crossing of the Red Sea in Exodus may be placed in this category. Absolute miracles are those which are totally different from the usual processes of nature, such as the raising of the dead. Further, there needs to be a distinction between *Divine* and *Satanic* miracles.[99]

There should also be an interpretive distinction between that in the Scriptures which represents the *ideal goal* of the spiritual life and that which is *realizable*. If those Biblical statements which indicate the unattainable ideal are explained as if they represent the attainable, many problems will result. For a case in point see Matthew 5:48.

S.   One should carefully avoid intermingling evaluation with interpretation. Value-judgments should be withheld until the meaning of a passage has been ascertained. What a man is saying must first be discovered before it can be adjudged whether what he says is right or wrong. This principle cannot be overemphasized.[100]

T.   One should also abstain from apologetics before exposition has been completed. In fact, if the meaning of a unit is really discovered, it will need no defense. For the release of the Scriptures is itself the best polemic in their favor.

U.   It is not to be assumed that when one has followed the procedures heretofore discussed, one's expositions will inevitably be final and immutable. Such might be the case if the suggestions were ideally practiced. However, since few things are done ideally, allowance should be made for altering one's interpretations if and when it becomes necessary. In fact, in a real sense explanations which result from true inductive study are always tentative, since they are subject to change whenever new evidence is brought to light through a further examination of the particulars.[101]

V.   Someone has called attention to the fact that there are two kinds of knowledge. The one is horizontal knowledge, which is encyclopedic in nature. The other is vertical knowledge, which involves depth rather than scope. Thus, for instance, a person who is aware of the various attributes of God and is able to define them in terms of their basic meaning has the first type of knowledge. He knows, for example, that God is holy and good and eternal and loving, and he is acquainted with the primary definitions of these qualities. When, however, through various means he delves into the profound implications of each of these as well as their relations to each other, his knowledge becomes vertical. It is this vertical kind of knowledge which ought to be the final goal of the Biblical interpreter.

There are various ways of developing a vertical knowledge of the Scriptures. One means is to acquire a wide acquaintance with theological and philosophical thought. Contact with outstanding minds like those of Plato, Origen, and Augustine will make one aware of the deeper meaning of the great ideas with which the Scriptures are concerned. Even from a negative point of view a cognizance of various theological and philosophical positions enhances one's insight into the deeper signification of Scriptural truth. For instance, when one contrasts the point of view of Genesis 1 to atheism, polytheism, materialism, pantheism, deism, fatalism, Gnosticism, humanism, rationalism, existentialism, etc., one begins to discern the profound implications of the first chapter of Genesis. In fact, it is salutary to possess a basic knowledge of other areas of study such as psychology and sociology in order to understand the significance of Biblical statements in those areas. A wide acquaintance, then, with theological, philosophical, psychological, and sociological thought and problems awakens the mind so that it is prepared to grasp the profound truths of the Scriptures, and vertical knowledge is the consequence. One cannot come to the

Bible with a blank or lethargic mind and expect to drink of its deep waters.

However, there is another essential means which must be considered. One must also spend much time in prayerful meditation if one is to fathom the depths of the Scriptures. The interpreter should therefore discipline himself to spend an hour or more thinking about one particular truth or passage. In such periods of meditation it is often helpful to write down the thoughts which come to one's attention. When one practices this concentrated type of reflection, one will begin perceiving the underlying meaning of Biblical truth. One will also begin seeing the relations and interrelations between truths and thereby discover the unity of truth.

W. One should make it a point to read histories of interpretation, such as that by Farrar or Grant. Histories of the English Bible, such as those by Baikie and Goodspeed, also provide a valuable means of enhancing one's ability to expound the Scriptures.

VI. SUMMARY OF INTERPRETATION

The function of the interpreter is so to empathize with Biblical authors and characters that he is able to relive their experiences. This is accomplished through the use of the imagination, by which there occurs a mental and spiritual transference to Scriptural situations which makes possible their re-creation.

Such re-creation transcends the mere discovery of the basic meaning of Biblical expressions. For Biblical writers and characters had reasons for their statements, including certain motives for making them in a given literary and historical context. Moreover, Scriptural statements implicate certain unexpressed facts, some of which they presuppose and some of which are their logical outgrowth. Thus if interpretation is to be truly re-creative, it must involve rational and implicational aspects as well as that of definition.

The specific process by which such re-creative interpretation is accomplished contains three major parts: first, *interpretive questions,* which are based on one's observations and which express in interrogative form the phases involved in their re-creative exposition; second, *answers* to these questions, which are determined primarily by the nature and requirements of the Scriptures themselves; and third, the *integration and summarization* of these answers so as to discover the essential message of the thought unit.

In all this the efficient expositor will be analytical, discriminating, thorough, methodical, and sincere. For it is his responsible and solemn task to interpret God's revelation to men, upon which hangs their eternal destiny.

VII. EXERCISE ON INTERPRETATION

In the case of each passage studied in connection with the preceding exercise, attempt to determine which questions are essential. Then make an effort to answer those and as many others as you can. In connection with each question, examine the various exegetical determinants to ascertain which ones may be applicable to it. Then discover what each contributes to its answer, if anything. After you have done as thorough a piece of independent work as possible in a reasonable length of time, consult the various commentaries on the passage. Then integrate your answers and use one or more of the means of summarization suggested. Thoughout the project make a conscious effort to utilize the principles and suggestions of the preceding discussion.

NOTES

1. Coulton, G. G., *Five Centuries of Religion*, Volume I, p. xxxi.
2. It would do the reader much good to peruse the entire first chapter of L. Gilman's *Toscanini and Great Music*. The reading of this chapter will help explain why in a book on Bible study so much reference is made to Toscanini.
3. *Webster's Collegiate Dictionary*, Fifth Edition.
4. Ibid.
5. Ewen, D., *The Story of Arturo Toscanini*.
6. The term "rational" connotes that which concerns reasons; it does not imply that which is reasonable in contrast to what is unreasonable. This also applies to the interpretive question described by the same term. (Post, pp. 104ff.)
7. Some of these implications become evident when one examines such passages as Matthew 22:34-40, I Corinthians 13, and James 2:1-13.
8. The use of the question in this connection is suggested because it is more effective than the mere consideration of the different aspects of interpretation. For the interrogative form seems to bring these aspects to a sharper focus than is otherwise possible. Furthermore, a question has a way of demanding an answer; it haunts the mind until a reply is given. It is for these and other reasons that Jesus frequently used the principle of interrogation in His ministry. Because of these facts the interpretive question is deemed an important tool for Biblical exegesis.
9. Interpretive questions are expressions of curiosity. Coleridge once said that "philosophy begins in wonder." The same may be said of insight into the meaning of Biblical statements. In this connection, note that interpretive questions represent the adaptation of the Socratic question to the field of Bible study. Consequently, if the reader is interested in gaining a better understanding of the important role of interpretive questions in relation to the Bible, let him study the Socratic dialogues of Plato.

10. Ante, p. 39. The observational question as applied to structural relations may be called the "analytical" question, since its purpose is to cause one to analyze the function of one part of a passage in relation to its other parts and to the whole.

11. The reason for the inclusion of illustrations for each category of interpretive questions is not so much the writer's passion for thoroughness as his hope that they will elucidate in some measure this important aspect of methodical study.

12. Observation was defined in its ideal sense at the outset so as to include an awareness of the need to explain the particulars which are noted. (Ante, pp. 31-32.) However, experience has shown that one may be conscious of the presence of a term or a structural relation and yet not actually realize the need for its exposition. It is for this reason that there is an emphasis on the use of interpretive questions to make one aware of the need for discovering *meaning as well as forms.*

13. Ante, pp. 68-71.

14. On the basis of the statements made regarding explanatory questions in the areas of general literary forms and atmosphere, it is easy to surmise that the various types of definitive questions do not have equal value. Those which concern terms and structural relations are more significant than those in the spheres of literary form and atmosphere. This is generally true in regard to rational and implicational questions as well. For in a sense one needs to know the answers to interpretive questions about literary forms or atmosphere before one can intelligently use them in the observation of a passage. For example, one's characterization of a portion as poetry necessitates an awareness of the meaning of the poetic form if it is done with understanding. On the other hand, we humans have a tendency to use descriptive terms without an exact knowledge of what they mean. It is because of this tendency that the interpretive questions which concern general literary forms and underlying tone are of value.

15. Ante, p. 96.

16. Note that selectivity may be observed both in connection with the writer himself and the characters involved in his writing. In this instance the selectivity of the author presupposes the selectivity of Jesus.

17. The answer to this question provides an example of an implicit structural relation. (Ante, pp. 38-39.)

18. Ante, p. 100.

19. Because of the brevity of the discussion of form-al and atmospheric questions, they will sometimes be combined. The same will apply to some of the other more minor types of questions.

20. Ante, pp. 68-71; also post, pp. 148-150.

21. Ibid.

22. Psalm 23 was chosen for this study for three primary reasons: because of its brevity, because of its familiarity, and because it is a structural entity.

23. As was noted heretofore, some observations, especially in the sphere of structure, cannot be made until a certain amount of interpretation has occurred. It is to make one aware of the need for such observations that the observational or analytical question is introduced among the interpretive questions. All of the observational questions used will concern structural relations. (Ante, pp. 99-100.)

24. Because the Psalm is poetic in form and consequently employs figurative language, the problem of interpretation is twofold: first, to discover what is involved in the physical basis of the imagery, which in this instance means determining the qualities of a physical shepherd of physical sheep; and second, to decide wherein the metaphors are applicable to the realm of the spirit, that is, to discover wherein Jehovah's character and His relation to the Psalmist is like a shepherd's character and his relation to his sheep. In order to discover this twofold meaning, interpretive questions should be asked both in regard to the physical images and to their spiritual counterparts. The reader will note that in this instance questions were suggested in both of these realms. However, those concerned with the physical image will generally be assumed to conserve space.

INTERPRETATION   193

25. "Shepherd" and "Sheep," when capitalized, indicate the spiritual application of the physical image.

26. Similar questions may be asked regarding another structural relation if the answer to the first question in the series is "no." This holds true elsewhere in the exercise.

27. Since the entire Psalm is involved in a question such as this, the component of the passage is omitted from its classification.

28. For a technical analysis of the literary form of Psalm 23, see Delitzsch, F., *A Commentary on the Psalms, Volume I,* ad. loc. The over-all structure of the Psalm will be found in chart form in the Appendix. For this reason it is not reviewed at this point in the exercise. (Ante, p. 72.)

29. Ante, p. 9.

30. Ante, pp. 69-70.

31. Ante, pp. 20-21.

32. Ante, p. 16.

33. Ante, p. 72.

34. Ante, pp. 31-32, 74, 77-79.

35. Ante, p. 49.

36. Ante, p. 75.

37. Ante, p. 73.

38. Ante, p. 100.

39. Ante, p. 20.

40. All of these passages are not complete literary units. Some of them were purposely curtailed in order to encourage a more thorough listing of observations and interpretive questions.

41. Both Paul and Jesus were calling attention to a factor which is important in any teacher-student relationship. If learning does not occur, one of two things may be the cause: either the teacher is at fault, or the student is not receptive or is otherwise incapable of being taught.

42. Ante, p. 13. It was because of an awareness of the indispensability of the spiritual factor that it was included among the basic premises of methodical study. For what is necessary for the achievement of a goal is a logical part of any means designed for reaching it.

43. If this discussion were intended to be exhaustive, it would

need to treat thoroughly the general problem of the place of reason in the exegetical process. Since, however, it is merely suggestive, suffice it to say that the statements on common sense imply that the rational factor is a significant ingredient in the interpretive process. And this fact is important to recognize, for in some instances "revelation" and "faith" have been so defined so as to exclude the reason.

44. Some of the following exegetical factors cannot be fully utilized without some knowledge of the original. Therefore, if the reader does not know the original languages, he is urged to learn at least how to recognize the consonants and vowels so that he may utilize dictionaries and lexicons. Of course, a thorough knowledge of the original languages is to be commended most highly.

45. It is a significant fact that the examination of the comparative usage of words within the Scriptures, which is of great importance in their interpretation, may be accomplished for the most part on the basis of the vernacular.

46. The study of the usage of words within the Scriptures actually involves the factor of contextual relations, which will be considered a few pages hence. (Post, pp. 145-148.)

47. It is frequently forgotten that matters of etymological background and comparative usage are important in a study of the vernacular as well as in the examination of the original. For presumably those who translated the Scriptures were aware of the root meaning, derivative significance, and usage of the terms which they utilized. If this be true, then a good English dictionary should also be one of the tools in the methodical study of the English Bible. This same principle applies to other interpretive factors such as inflections and syntax, in connection with which grammatical discussions of the English language may be validly employed.

48. Terry, M. S., *Biblical Hermeneutics*, p. 86.

49. Ante, p. 35. It should be noted that various factors mentioned in the chapter on observation will be treated again in this connection. Among these are literal and figurative terms, inflections, structure, general literary forms, and atmosphere. It may appear at first glance that this

entails needless repetition. However, there are certain reasons why it is necessary to recall these factors at this juncture.

For one thing, an effort is being made to present *all* of the major determinants which may be utilized in answering *any* interpretive question. Thus, for instance, one may have observed the terms "desolating sacrilege" in Mark 13:14. On the basis of this term-al observation, one may have asked: "What is meant by 'desolating sacrilege'? Why are these terms used here?" In answering these questions one will utilize some of the factors mentioned in the preceding pages, such as etymology and usage. However, it may also be necessary to bring to bear the structural relation of interrogation, which is basic to the framework of the passage. Now even if it were true that one had observed this relation in the first place, which is not necessarily the case, it does not follow that its observation would lead automatically to an insight into its interpretive significance or to its automatic use in the interpretive process. For one may observe the law of interrogation in Mark 13 and never realize that it has a bearing on the interpretation of "desolating sacrilege" in view of the fact that these terms appear in Jesus' answer to specific questions of the disciples. Thus for the sake of thoroughness one must mention these factors again, for they all interact to make exposition possible.

Moreover, even in relation to those instances when the interaction of the factors does not occur, the very process of interpretation itself demands the restatement of each. For example, one may observe the present inflection of the verb "is revealed" in Romans 1:18. On the basis of such an observation, one may raise the following questions: "What is involved in the present tense? Why is it used here?" What, then, determines how one shall answer these questions? The primary factor is the nature and significance of the Greek present tense. Thus the movement is as follows: first, the observation of the tense; second, interpretive questions regarding the tense; and third, interpretive answers based on an analysis of the present tense—

its types, uses, and significance. In other words, *certain factors are seen in observation for the purpose of analyzing them and applying them in interpretation.* Thus the factor of inflection and other similar factors appear both in the observational process and in the interpretive process. *The correlation between these two phases of study is necessary* if one's approach is to be methodical.

A third reason for the restatement of these factors is to indicate more thoroughly their interpretive significance. This was done somewhat in the discussion of observation in order to clarify the reason why these factors should be noted in the first place. However, there is the need to demonstrate their exegetical import more fully if this discussion is to be meaningful.

And finally, frequently the discovery of some of these factors will not occur until one is engaged in the process of answering interpretive questions. Therefore, if one did not call attention to them in this phase of study, they might be overlooked to the detriment of valid interpretation.

50. See the Appendix for an abbreviated example of a word study involving some of these factors.

51. Ante, pp. 35-36. The identity of terms is assumed here, since for one thing only certain types of terms have certain inflections.

52. Dana and Mantey, *A Manual Grammar of the Greek New Testament,* p. 197.

53. These statements do not imply that inflections have the same significance in every language. For each language has its peculiar characteristics. For example, the tenses of English verbs primarily involve the time element; the tense of Hebrew verbs have nothing to do with time, but are rather concerned with states of action; the tenses of Greek verbs are very similar to those of the Hebrew, although they include somewhat of the time element. Thus each language is individual, and one should never make the mistake of treating them as identical. There must be an attempt to relate them to each other, especially because of the use of the English translation. But this should be done

with an awareness of their marked differences. (Ante, p. 81.)

54. Ante, pp. 40-55.

55. All of these contextual factors are not present in connection with every term of every passage.

56. Ante, pp. 68-71.

57. For a more thorough discussion of the interpretive significance of the parabolic form, see the opening chapters of R. Trench's *Notes on the Parables of Our Lord*.

58. "Revelation, Book of," *Schaff-Herzog Encyclopedia of Religious Knowledge*.

59. Ante, p. 71.

60. Ante, pp. 93-95.

61. Included in this aspect are all those factors of higher criticism concerned with the writing of Biblical books.

   One of the many examples of the importance of historical background for interpretation is the need to know the views of Gnosticism is order to understand fully Colossians and I John.

62. Ante, pp. 10-11, 93-95. The psychological factor is relevant to the controversy as to whether Jesus conceived Himself to be the greatest of the prophets or whether He thought of Himself as Divine. In this connection Jesus' sayings and actions, such as the statements of Matthew 11:27-30, should be compared with those of the prophets to discover whether the self-consciousness expressed by them is essentially the same or qualitatively different.

   For another example of the outworking of the psychological factor, see pages 17-22 of the pamphlet *Neglected Emphases in Biblical Criticism,* which contains Dr. Donald G. Miller's inaugural address as Walter H. Robertson Professor of New Testament at Union Theological Seminary, Richmond, Virginia.

   This exegetical principle has engaged the endeavors of Dr. A. C. Wyckoff, recently retired from The Biblical Seminary in New York. Dr. Wyckoff has done an outstanding piece of work in this field, and the writer is greatly indebted to him for whatever insight he may have into its interpretive significance.

63. Ante, p. 96. The rational and implicational phases of interpretation are both involved in this factor.
64. Post, p. 160.
65. Post, pp. 206-208, 212-213.
66. See Galatians 4:4.
67. See the inclusion of the aorist form of "receive" in Mark 11:24 for an example of the operation of the latter procedure. Also note that, strictly speaking, the consideration of textual criticism properly belongs in the section on observation, since it concerns the observational question, "What is here?" However, because among other things it is sometimes necessary to expound the context in order to decide which variant reading is most in keeping with it, it seems wise to treat this matter under interpretation.
68. Dana, H. E., *Searching the Scriptures*, p. 237.
69. Ante, pp. 8-9.
70. Ante, pp. 21-22. It should be noted that though the factor of exegetical opinion is classified as an objective determinant, since it is indeed objective in relation to the individual student, it does have a subjective element in it from the standpoint of the commentator.
71. Ante, pp. 20-21.
72. Ante, p. 16.
73. Ante, p. 77.
74. See the Appendix for a discussion of logical outlines.
75. The paraphrase may also be employed in the application of Scriptural truth. Some of the Psalms and certain passages from the prophets especially lend themselves to this kind of treatment.
76. Consult the Appendix for illustrations.
77. The following types of interpretation have been called by different names and have been organized in various ways. In fact, some of the terms used in this discussion are employed by others in the opposite sense. Therefore, the nomenclature utilized here must be understood in the light of its context.
78. Ante, pp. 145-148. The way to avoid this dangerous practice in preaching is to conceive of the sermon as an ex-

position of a structural unit of the Scriptures. Such sermons are called "expository" sermons.

79. Ante, pp. 6-8, 11-12.
80. Ante, pp. 136-137.
81. Ante, p. 69.
82. Ante, pp. 70-71, 148-149.
83. Ante, pp. 93-95, 152.
84. Ante, pp. 142-143. The writer is not necessarily implying that he accepts the figurative view of Genesis 3. He is simply stating that it is possible to accept a figurative interpretation and still retain a belief in its essential historicity.
85. Whether the third use of the Old Testament is essentially different from the second may be debatable; however, the writer has found the distinction between them to be helpful.
86. The use which the New Testament makes of Old Testament examples lends support to this view. See, for instance, Hebrews 3-4.
87. Note that the systematic approach, like some of the others, tends to move beyond interpretation to evaluation, application, and correlation, which are the next phases of methodical study.
88. Ante, pp. 140-141.
89. Ante, pp. 9-10.
90. This list of erroneous types of interpretation is not exhaustive, for it does not include such types as mystical interpretation or the moral interpretation of Kant. Nor does it involve mutually exclusive elements.

Incidentally, the reader undoubtedly wonders why the facts mentioned above are constantly stressed in regard to the various illustrations and classifications given. This practice is followed because the writer has found that students frequently assume that whenever a list is presented it is meant to exhaust all the possibilities, and that any attempt to classify different elements necessarily implies that the categories are mutually exclusive. Such assumptions have often led to misunderstandings and problems. Therefore, in order to avoid similar errors in interpreta-

tion, the above-mentioned facts are brought constantly to
the reader's attention.

91. Terry, M. S., *Biblical Hermeneutics*, p. 101.
92. Ante, pp. 152-154.
93. Ante, pp. 156-158.
94. Ante, p. 11.
95. Ante, pp. 96, 155-156.
96. Ante, pp. 179-180.
97. Ante, p. 167.
98. Ante, pp. 170-171, 174-175.
99. For a more thorough discussion of these distinctions, see
the opening section of R. Trench's *Notes on the Miracles*.
100. In this connection see Greene, T. M., *The Arts and the
Art of Criticism*, pp. 369-373.
101. Ante, pp. 21-22.

Evaluation and Application

CHAPTER THREE

Evaluation and Application

Evaluation and Application [1]

HAVING DISCOVERED THE meaning of a Biblical passage, the next logical step is to ascertain what values may be derived from it for the edification of life. This step necessarily involves two phases, which have been termed "evaluation" and "application."

It will be impossible to discuss the many intricacies of this step of study. Therefore, the purpose of the forthcoming presentation will be to set forth some essential principles and outline the main aspects involved in evaluating and applying Biblical statements. The details must be left for the reader himself to work out.

I. EVALUATION

A. Meaning and Place of Evaluation

To evaluate is to assess the worth of something, to appraise its excellence, relevance, and usefulness. Thus the process of evaluation involves answering questions such as these: "Is an author successful or not in what he attempts to do? How well does he accomplish his purpose? Are his statements valid or invalid? If valid, for whom and when and for what purposes are they valid?" [2]

In view of the meaning of evaluation, two facts should be stressed regarding its proper place in methodical study. The first was stated at the close of the discussion on interpretation, namely, that evaluation must follow interpretation and not precede it or be simultaneous with it.[3] The second fact is that evaluation must precede application proper. Contrary to common belief and practice, a Scriptural unit is not ready to apply as soon as its meaning has been discovered. Interpretation needs to be followed by a process of assessment whereby the relevance and worth of a passage are ascertained before its employment can have a valid foundation. In fact, evaluation may well be considered the major phase of the general process of application. For the haphazard employment of Scriptural statements without their prior evaluation may lead to spiritual disaster. On the other hand, if proper appraisal occurs, then valid application is well on its way.

There should therefore be no attempt to exempt the Scriptures from judicial criticism.[4] For individual parts of the Bible have varying degrees of pertinence and value. This is illustrated by the fact that if one could possess only certain books of the Scriptures, there are those which one would prefer above others. There undoubtedly would be a difference of opinion as to which specific books should be chosen, but the fact remains that a choice would be made, a choice which presupposes a variety of worth. These facts merely serve to emphasize the truth that to avoid the legitimate evaluation of Biblical units, as many do, is unreasonable. The appraisal of Scriptural passages ought rather to be practiced faithfully in order that Bible study shall have its proper culmination.

B. Process of Evaluation

1. Process of General Evaluation

In the evaluation of Biblical statements one is concerned with two major questions. The first of these involves the general validity and worth of the Scriptures as a whole or of large parts of them. It may be stated thus: "Is the Bible (or a major part of the Bible) of any value for the modern man, or is it invalid and worthless?"

This question is basic to all Scriptural evaluation and application. For if the answer to it is to the effect that the Bible as a whole or a large portion of it is of no value for contemporary life, then the process of evaluation has been completed in relation to the material in question, and further, the possibility of application has been removed, since the presupposition of application is that Biblical statements have value and therefore should be employed for the improvement of life.

The process involved in answering this basic question is too complex for detailed treatment in this book. However, in general it involves applying all of the tests of truth and value which may be utilized in ascertaining the veracity and worth of any metaphysical or purportedly historical statement. In relation to metaphysics such tests would include among others the pragmatic test and that of congruity. With regard to the historicity of the Scriptures, one may use all the tests applied in a court of law to decide what events actually occurred. Among other things, these would involve determining the genuineness of the documents and the reliability of the witnesses, evaluating corroborating evidence, and judging the psychological soundness of Biblical statements.[5]

2. Process of Specific Evaluation

Assuming that one's answer to the first problem is to the effect that the Scriptures are generally valuable for contemporary life, one is confronted by the second major question of evaluation. It is more specific in nature and may be phrased thus: "Since the Bible is of value for contemporary life, what is the exact worth of the statements of particular passages? When and where and for whom are they worthwhile?"

The primary task of this phase of evaluation is to analyze the statements of a passage in order to determine which of its truths are timeless and therefore of contemporary worth. This implies that because the books of the Bible were written at certain points in history and were adapted to their settings, some of their statements are local and therefore restricted in their value. A distinction must therefore be made between those truths which are local and those which are general. For to employ local truths as if they were general would be to invite trouble in the field of application.

The Scriptures themselves indicate that the ultimate standard for determining which truths are universal is Jesus Christ, who, as the Incarnate Son of God, embodies that which is of timeless and supreme value. All things must therefore be measured by Him. Thus, since the New Testament contains His life and its implications, it becomes the grounds for appraising the statements of the Old Testament.

The specific process involved in determining which truths are universal will now be illustrated in relation to the three main types of passages which one confronts.

The first type consists of Old Testament passages, especially those of the pre-prophetic era, which contain restricted truths because they were written in the earlier stages of a developing revelation.[6] One may cite Deuteronomy 27-30 as an example of this kind.

In interpreting this passage one discovers its main message to be that physical and spiritual blessing will come to the Israelites if they obey God; on the other hand, if they disobey Him, they will receive physical and spiritual judgment. This is borne out by the contrasting lists of blessings and curses in chapters 27-28, as well as by the summary paragraph at the conclusion of chapter 30.

Since this passage is found in the *Old* Testament, which has been transcended by the *New* Testament because it contains God's final and supreme revelation to man in Jesus Christ, one must appraise Deuteronomy 27-30 on the basis of the New Testament. When one does this one discovers that some of the truths of this passage are local and restricted in nature. For the New Testament believer is not promised both physical and spiritual prosperity because he becomes a disciple of Christ. On the contrary, the New Testament clearly teaches that often physical adversity will accompany discipleship. For some examples of this teaching, see Matthew 5:10-12, Luke 6:20-26, John 15:20-27, and the book of the Acts.

Moreover, the very death of Jesus Himself is the supreme contradiciton of the inevitable relation between physical and spiritual prosperity. For though Jesus was the Son of God and the spiritual Messiah, He was not the physical Messiah whom some expected. Rather He proclaimed His function to be that of becoming a spiritual redeemer through physical death. And what is more, He demanded a similar outlook on the part of His disciples; for He said to them, "If any man would come after me, let him deny himself and take up his cross and follow me." (Mark 8:34)

The New Testament thus makes a clear-cut distinction between physical and spiritual blessing which is not found in Deuteronomy 27-30 and which would not have been understood by most of the people of Old Testament times. This is substantiated by an examination of those Old Testament passages which represent the beginning of the dissociation of the physical and the spiritual which culminates in the New Testament. Take, for example, Isaiah 53. Its beginning is significant: "Who hath believed our message? and to whom hath the arm of the Lord been revealed?" The concept of a suffering servant was incredible to those who heard it. For how could a servant of God suffer? In fact, the Pharisees of Jesus' day manifested the same unbelief because they also failed to distinguish between the spiritual and the physical.

Now it does not follow that because the New Testament separates physical and spiritual blessing, Deuteronomy 27-30 contains no general truth which is of value to our times. For there was a reason for the association of the physical and the spiritual in Deuteronomy. Physical blessings were tokens of spiritual blessings. Their presence was needed to teach the people that God keeps His word, and that obedience to Him is the secret of Israel's well-being. However, with the coming of Christ these symbols were no longer needed. The Incarnation itself became the Symbol by which men are taught that God is faithful to His promises, and that eternal life depends on one's relation to Him. Thus the basic teaching of Deuteronomy 27-30 and the New Testament is *essentially* the same. The difference between them is one of means rather than end, and it becomes apparent when one examines the teaching of Jesus that the road to eternal life may well be the road of total physical self-sacrifice. For He said to those about Him, "Whosoever would save his life shall lose it; and whosoever shall lose his life for my sake and the gospel's shall save it. For what doth it profit a man, to gain the whole world and forfeit his life?" (Mark 8:35-36) '

A second type of passage one finds as one attempts to ascertain which Biblical truths are universal is that which contains references to certain local situations and practices. Romans 14:1-15:13, I Corinthians 11:1-16, and Galatians 5 are examples of this kind.

If one examines the first of these, Romans 14:1-15:13, one finds that it concerns certain local problems of the Roman Church, such as the quarrel between those who ate meat and those who did not. Now this problem as such has little relevance for most of us, not because of its inherent nature but simply because of its obsolescence. However, in dealing with it Paul enunciates certain basic principles which in view of the whole New Testament are timeless and thus of great relevance to us. These may be summarized in the following words: there is a certain peripheral area in a Christian's experience in which his conscience alone should be the authority as to whether or not a particular practice should be followed; and in determining what his decision shall be, he should be guided by two primary factors, namely, his faith-relation to God and his consequent concern for his fellowmen.

Thus in relation to such a passage when one merely removes the accidents, that is, those practices or situations which have a local flavor, and finds that which is foundational, one discovers the truths which have universal relevance and worth.

A third type of passage is that which, though addressed to a concrete historical situation, contains statements which could well be addressed to anyone. John 3:16-21 fits into this category. In fact, when judged on the basis of New Testament standards, some Old Testament passages such as Isaiah 53 may be classified in this group.

The reader should not infer that the preceding groups are rigid. There are many ramifications and variations. Some passages combine elements of the various types. Other classifications could be devised. But the main point of the discussion remains, namely, that one must distinguish between those truths which are local and restricted in contrast to those which are timeless and general if application is to have a proper foundation.[8]

C. Miscellaneous Suggestions for Evaluation

The following list of suggestions is concerned with both the general problem of evaluation and with some of its more specific aspects.

1. In the process of evaluation one should persistently abstain from snap judgments. One's appraisal should be characterized by deliberate decisions and a suspension of judgment whenever necessary. One should be more ready to doubt the value of one's judgment than the value of a particular Scriptural unit. For there is great

reason to suspect that there is much more to certain parts of the Bible than sometimes meets the eye if it is remembered that the Scriptures have survived centuries of derogatory criticism and persecution. And they have not survived without sufficient cause. They must have great survival value! The safest policy in appraising certain statements, then, is to be exceedingly slow in adjudging them to be worthless.

2. One should beware of the entrance of the subjective element into evaluation. There is the real danger that one's appraisal may reflect one's desires and may therefore serve as a means of attempting to escape responsibility.

3. The work of every author should be evaluated primarily on the basis of his purpose. If, for example, a writer is attempting to describe the making of an atom bomb, he cannot reasonably be censured for not giving the recipe for pumpkin pie. Or if an author has written a modern historical novel, he cannot be criticized for failing to include in it the fall of Rome. Once the purpose of a work has been discovered, one's evaluation must be guided by it. For it is assumed that every author has a right to self-limitation; and provided his self-limitation is valid, he must be judged solely on the basis of it.

4. Judicial criticism must take into account the historical situation in which the events of a passage occurred or to which it was addressed. A Biblical unit should not be evaluated merely on the basis of an abstract or universal standard, even though such a standard be found in the New Testament. Proper appraisal will involve a consideration of the exigencies, the limitations, and the requirements of the concrete historical setting of a passage before there is any final attempt to pronounce it right or wrong, good or bad.

This principle is especially applicable to the ethics of the Old Testament, which are often judged solely on the grounds of an ideal New Testament standard. One should remember that moral codes change and should therefore distinguish between the goodness of a particular event or idea for those in its original setting and for those who live in the era of the New Testament. For there is the possibility that a certain practice may be pronounced good when judged on the basis of its contemporary criteria, but bad when evaluated by present standards. Although the latter appraisal is most important and the final one, it should be founded upon the former.

For, in fact, if indiscriminate judgment is passed on Biblical units, it may be forgotten that in specific instances the motivation of a particular action may have been and may still be good, whereas its concrete outworking, though valid in the past, may be deemed wrong when measured by the higher criteria of the present. One's zeal for God, for instance, may have expressed itself in an unjust manner in terms of modern standards. This fact, however, does not negate the desirability of zeal for God.

For several reasons, then, one ought to make a legitimate distinction between the merit of a practice to those who originally engaged in it and for the modern Christian; and this distinction, which is based on an awareness of the historical setting of the Scriptures, should be kept in mind throughout the process of evaluation.

5. One should be consistent in one's evaluations. One should not pronounce something good in a certain instance, and adjudge the same thing to be bad under similar conditions. On the other hand, if one censures an action or an idea in a given situation, one should not condone it in a comparable situation. There are many who condemn the practices of certain parts of the Old Testament and at the same time approve essentially the same practices in the modern world.

6. The most important judgment in regard to those passages which purport to be historical concerns whether they are in reality historical or whether they are unhistorical. Such an appraisal is much more significant, for example, than the interpretive decision regarding the literary nature of a unit, that is, whether it is literal or figurative.[9]

7. In evaluating those parts of the Bible in which there are seeming discrepancies, it should be remembered that even if the discrepancies are real, they are not substantial but accidental in nature.[10] The significance of this distinction becomes clearer when one examines the meaning of "substance" and "accident." "Substance" may be defined thus:

That which underlies all outward manifestations; real, unchanging essence or nature; that in which qualities, or accidents, inhere; that which constitutes anything what it is. Essential element or elements . . .

In fact, etymologically speaking, the word "substance" derives from the Latin *substare*, which means "to be under or present, to stand firm." An "accident," on the other hand, is a "contingent circumstance . . . A quality, especially one not in the essence or specific nature of a thing." It comes from the Latin *accidere*, which means "to happen." [11]

Thus by indicating that possible variations in the Bible are accidental rather than substantial, one implies that they concern its contingents but do not touch that which is necessary to its nature. Therefore, they can in no way alter the basic worth of the Scriptures because in spite of them the Scriptures remain what they are.

That such a distinction between accidents and substance is legitimate may easily be demonstrated from everyday life. For example, one may enter a forest which contains many elm trees. They all have in common that underlying quality which makes them elm trees rather than some other kind of tree. They are therefore substantially the same. However, in regard to accidentals they will undoubtedly differ. Some will be taller than others; some will have more branches than others. But these variations in no way alter the fact that they are still elm trees and nothing else. Similarly, there often occur errors in birth certificates. At times the date or place of birth is not recorded accurately. However, this by no means changes the fact that the person involved was born. And it is this fact which is essential and of supreme importance. The inaccuracy of the birth certificate is purely accidental.

It should be emphasized that though some Scriptural variations may actually exist, many of them are found to be apparent rather than real when they are examined closely. In this connection Terry writes:

A large proportion of the discrepancies of the Bible are traceable to one or more of the following causes: the errors of copyists in the manuscripts; the variety of names applied to the same person or place; different methods of reckoning times and seasons; and the special scope and plan of each particular book. Variations are not contradictions, and many variations arise from different methods of arranging a series of particular facts. The peculiarities of oriental thought and speech often involve seeming extravagance of statement and verbal inaccuracies, which are of a nature to provoke criticism of the less impassioned writers of the West.[12]

8. The accurate appraisal of the Scriptures must be based on an awareness of the history of their production, canonization, and transmission. The factors involved in this principle become abundantly clear when one studies histories of the Bible.[13]

II. APPLICATION

A. Process of Application

The applicatory step may be divided into two phases, each of which will now be discussed.

1. Analysis of Contemporary Situation in View of Passage

Having determined the universal elements of a passage through the process of evaluation, the next step is to discover the exact contemporary situation to which the passage is applicable. For though the truths one may have found are actually timeless, it does not follow that they can be applied indiscriminately to any circumstances.

Thus if one wants to apply the truth of a passage, one must either analyze a specific modern situation to ascertain whether it falls within the bounds of the universal truths, or one must find a contemporary situation which does. For example, if one is considering applying the timeless principle of Romans 14:1-15:13 to a certain practice,[14] one must first discover whether that practice may be validly classified as being peripheral, or whether it is central and essential in nature. For if the practice is substantial, then the employment of Romans 14:1-15:13 may lead to license rather than to true Christian freedom.

An excellent test in this regard is to compare the practice in question with the concrete situation to which Paul addressed his words. For that is peripheral which is fundamentally similar to eating or not eating meat; on the other hand, if a practice is essentially different from eating meat, then it is substantial rather than peripheral. Thus if the characteristics of the problem of eating meat are reflected in the modern problem, then the modern problem fits the situation of the passage in Romans. If, however, they are basically different, such as would be true if the modern problem were one of idolatry, then Paul's statements could not rightfully be applied to it.

2. Application of Passage

Theoretically, the application of a passage represents the sum total of the preceding two steps. For once one has discovered the universal truth of a passage as well as the contemporary situation which falls within its province, then one may bring the passage to bear on the situation, and the result is application. Thus one may compare the actual employment of a truth to discovering the numerical value of z in the formula $x + y = z$, once it is known that x equals one and y equals two.

There follows an illustration of this process based on Isaiah 55.

Prior Study (Interpretation of Main Message)—God will mercifully and abundantly forgive every captive Israelite who will truly repent of his sins and seek Him.

First Step (Specific Evaluation Based on New Testament: Universal Truth)—God will mercifully and abundantly forgive every sinner who will truly repent and seek Him.

Second Step (Contemporary Situation to Which Universal Truth Is Relevant)—You are sinners and you have truly repented and have sought God; or, you are sinners but you have not truly repented and sought God.

Third Step (Application Proper)—Therefore, God will mercifully and abundantly forgive you; or, therefore, God will not forgive you.[15]

Now of course the application of passages will not be as simple as this illustration and the preceding statements may make it appear; for inevitably one comes across various complications. But this discussion does illustrate the *basic* principles of application, especially in relation to the need and foundation for proper evaluation and the necessity for being certain that the modern situation belongs within the province of the passage being employed.

B. Kinds of Application

It should be realized that there are two distinct types of application: *theoretical* application and *practical* application. The first is a necessary foundation for the second; the second should be the logical outgrowth of the first.

There is the danger, however, that application may occur in the realm of concepts, and yet never be realized in the realm of deeds. One should be on one's guard against such a temptation, for to succumb to it will result in a mere lip service to the Scriptures which is not only worthless but detrimental.

C. Areas of Application

Biblical truths should be applied both personally and to others; they should be employed in connection with the political and economic aspects of life as well as the spiritual; they should be utilized locally, nationally, and universally; they should be applied to believers and to non-believers.

These are general statements and do not imply that the truths of each passage should be made applicable to all these areas of experience. For the very nature of the unit being studied is of supreme importance in determining the areas to which it should be applied. For example, certain portions of Scripture, like Romans 6, are relevant to believers and not to unbelievers.

Nevertheless, the practice of limiting applications to certain phases of experience can become a dangerous one. For example, there are some who always see wherein a Scriptural truth applies to others, whether it be other Christians or other nations; but they fail to relate the truth to their own personal or national life. On the other hand, some always apply truths to their own experiences and neglect their widespread implications for others. These and similar errors should be avoided. The applicatory process should be well rounded; it ought to include all the areas of life.

III. SUMMARY OF EVALUATION AND APPLICATION

The applicatory step is that for which all else exists. It represents the final purpose of Bible study.[16] However, if application is to be valid, it must be preceded by a process of evaluation.

Evaluation has both a general phase and a specific phase. In general, evaluation concerns itself with the worthwhileness of the Bible as a whole or major parts of it. Specifically, it involves determining the exact worth of particular passages. This latter phase is necessary because the books of the Bible were addressed to concrete historical situations and are therefore of varying relevance and value.

The major task of the specific phase of evaluation is to distinguish between those truths which are local and limited and those which are timeless and general. The basis for making such a distinction is the supreme and universal revelation which is embodied by Jesus Christ and which is recorded in the New Testament.

After the universal truth has been determined, one must then analyze a specific modern situation which may have occurred to one in order to ascertain whether it comes within the scope of the universal truth, or one must search for a contemporary problem to which the truth is relevant. When one has discovered a modern situation to which the timeless truth of the passage is pertinent, then it is one's duty to apply that truth, not only in concept but in deed. And one should apply it in whatever realm of life it is appropriate and regardless of the consequences. For in the last analysis one of the primary secrets of Scriptural application is the kind of abandon which causes one who has discovered a truth to follow it to its logical outcome, even if the road be hard and the tangible rewards few.

IV. EXERCISE ON EVALUATION AND APPLICATION

Consider the evaluation and application of those passages which you interpreted in connection with the preceding exercise. Try to follow the specific steps and general principles set forth in the preceding discussion.

NOTES

1. If one were attempting to follow scientific method precisely, one would insert at this point a further step which might be called "additional observation and experimentation." The implication of such a step would be that all initial interpretation is hypothetical, thus making further testing necessary. That this is true in a general sense no one can doubt; and in particular instances it is imperative that interpretation be considered tentative. However, the aforementioned step will not be included in this discussion for the simple reason that no attempt is being made to present a final approach to a Biblical unit. This was made clear at the outset of the manual, when it was stated that the pattern suggested in these pages is designed to be repeated in whole or in part, and further, that it makes allowance for interaction between the various steps. It has also been stressed that interpretations should always be subject to alteration if and when new data are discovered through additional observation. (Ante, pp. 21-22, 186.) Because of these facts, there seems to be no real need to treat "additional observation and experimentation" as a separate step in inductive Bible study.

2. At times the appraisal of a passage, especially in terms of its relevance to a given situation, is very closely related to interpretation, since it is the natural outgrowth of discovering the implications of Biblical statements. (Ante, p. 108.) However, since it involves a value-judgment, it must be distinguished from pure interpretation.

3. Ante, p. 186.
4. The expression "judicial criticism" is used in a neutral sense and in no way implies derogatory or destructive judgment. It is employed in the proper sense by T. M. Greene in *The Arts and the Art of Criticism.*
5. Ante, pp. 154-155. For bibliographical suggestions, see the opening sections of *A Bibliography of Systematic Theology for Theological Students,* compiled by the library of Princeton Theological Seminary.
6. Ante, pp. 156-158.
7. There are some who will maintain that Matthew 6:19-34 negates the position that the New Testament does not promise inevitable physical blessing to those who obey God. However, it is the writer's conviction that such a view is open to question both in terms of the statements of the passage itself and in terms of its relation to the other teachings of Christ and of the entire New Testament. It is true that often those who come to obey God have their needs supplied and, in fact, may fare better in some ways than before. However, this does not necessarily substantiate the concept of the *inevitable* relation between spiritual and physical well-being which predominates in some Old Testament passages.
8. At times the discovery of the underlying principles of a passage and therefore of its universal truth will occur during interpretation. This fact demonstrates again the flexibility of methodical study. (Ante, pp. 20-21.)
9. Ante, pp. 175-176.
10. The differences between the two lists of exiles in Ezra 2:1-70 and Nehemiah 7:6-73 may be cited as an example of an apparent variation.
11. *Webster's Collegiate Dictionary,* Fifth Edition.
12. Terry, M. S., *Biblical Hermeneutics,* p. 404.
13. Ante, p. 188.
14. Ante, pp. 208-209.
15. Note that Isaiah 55 belongs in the third type of passage previously discussed. (Ante, p. 209.)
16. Ante, pp. 12-13.

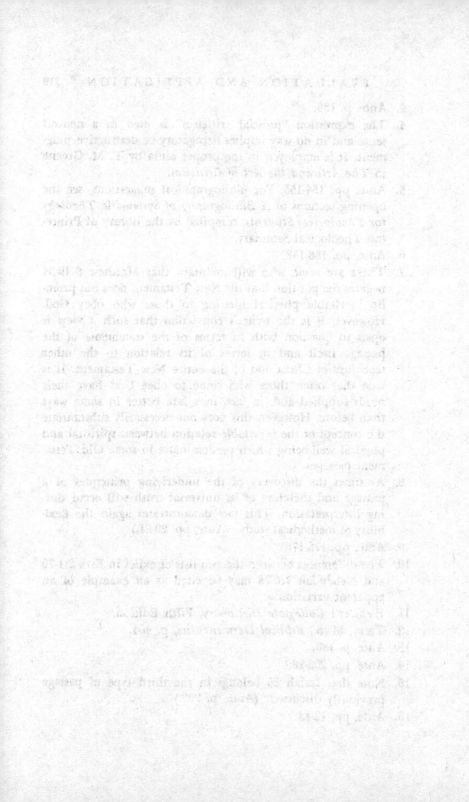

CHAPTER FOUR

Correlation

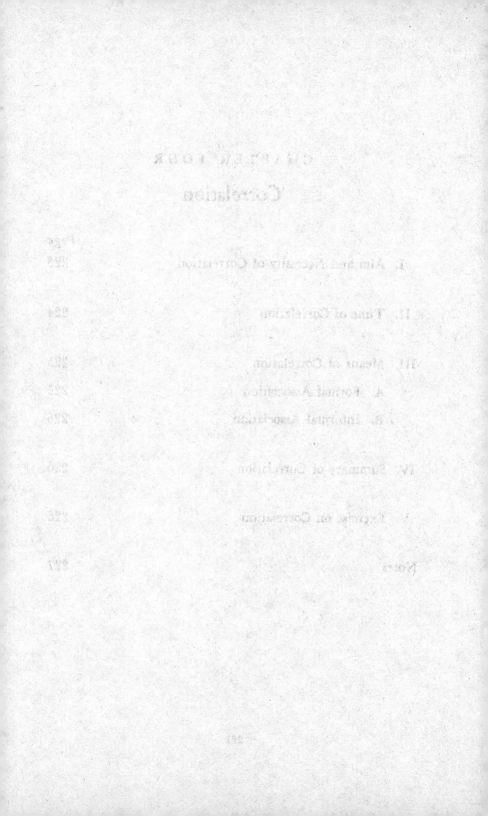

CHAPTER FOUR
Correlation

CHAPTER FOUR

Correlation

I. AIM AND NECESSITY OF CORRELATION

Although some correlation inevitably occurs during interpretation and application,[1] this phase forms the concluding step of the inductive study of the Scriptures. For it represents the generalizations which are the outgrowths of the examination of particular passages.[2]

To be more specific, the goal of Scriptural study is the development of a vital Biblical theology issuing in a vital Christian philosophy of life.[3] In order to accomplish this, one must do more than examine individual passages. One must coordinate one's findings so as to evolve a synthesized concept of the message of the Bible.[4] And having done this, one must attempt to relate it to those facts which one discovers outside the Scriptures.

There is no doubt but what the inductive approach to the Scriptures has been lacking at this very point. For just as deduction is strong in generalizations and weak in particulars, so induction tends to be strong in particulars and weak in generalization. The temptation is to spend so much time and energy studying individual passages that one never correlates what one has found.

Such a temptation must be overcome at all costs, for it is just as fallacious as laying a foundation and never building upon it. Generalization is the end of the examination of the particulars. And to neglect it is to fail in the accomplishment of one's objective, and what is more, to invite the criticism of those who insist that Bible study must be deductive if it is to be worthwhile.

II. TIME OF CORRELATION

The process of correlation cannot and need not wait until one has studied the entire Scriptures. This is true for four main reasons.

First, correlation, like all the other phases of inductive study, is ultimately tentative. There is always room for change if and when new data are discovered which warrant it. Thus one need not refrain from correlation because of the fear of forming immutable and deductive conclusions at the outset of one's study of the Scriptures.

Second, the study of the particulars ideally never ends. Therefore, correlation would never occur if it had to await the complete study of the particulars.

Third, there is a need to correlate parts of the Scriptures in order that one may guide one's thinking and actions. And since one needs to think and act in the present, correlation must commence in the present.

And fourth, the process of correlation is such a momentous task that it is best accomplished bit by bit rather than all at once. In fact, regardless of the method used, correlation is such a great strain on one's mental capacities that it is virtually an impossible intellectual feat in any ideal sense.

Thus the valid approach to correlation is to begin it soon after some passages have been studied and to continue it as long as one is able to think. It should be a lifetime process simultaneous with the continuous study of the particulars. For one will always discover new facts to synthesize, or gen-

eralizations which need revision because new evidence has
been found.

III. MEANS OF CORRELATION

There are two basic means which one may use to synthesize the discoveries made in the Scriptures with each other
and with the other data of experience.

A. Formal Association

This means involves correlation in terms of topics. Individual books of the Bible or the whole Bible may be surveyed in terms of their Theology, Anthropology, Soteriology,
Christology, Pneumatology, Ecclesiology, Ethics, etc. One
may also use these or similar topics by way of relating extra-
Biblical facts to the Scriptures.

Although the topical approach has certain advantages, it
also has some drawbacks. One of these is its tendency to
divide thought into superficial compartments, thus hinder-
ing one's awareness of the interrelatedness of truth.

B. Informal Association

This type of approach permits the association of passages
and facts whenever a relation exists between them and not
because they concern precisely the same topic. For example,
one may informally relate the truths of Mark 8:27-9:2,
John 15, and Romans 6:1-14. The first passage contains an
exhortation: "If any man would come after me, let him deny
himself and take up his cross and follow me." The latter
passages indicate the means by which this exhortation to
emulate Christ may be realized, namely, union with Christ
through faith which enables one to "abide" in Him. These
passages, which thus help to elucidate each other, might
never be associated if one were using solely the more formal
topical approach.

The informal approach is ultimately based on the principle that all truth and life are one. Every particular truth or phase of life has a natural affinity to every other truth or phase of life, both Scriptural and extra-Scriptural. One should therefore make a conscious effort to discover those ties which bind every fact to every other fact, and in so doing one will engage in the ideal expression of informal correlation.

Though to the writer's mind the latter approach is the most natural and valid, there are peculiar advantages to the topical approach from which one should benefit. In view of this, the reader is urged to use both means in his synthesis, always remembering, however, to avoid any artificial division of truth.[5]

IV. SUMMARY OF CORRELATION

Since this discussion is so brief, there is no real need to review its individual parts. However, it is worthwhile to call attention to its core, which is this: *always correlate.* One should constantly look for connections between various Biblical passages, and between Scriptural statements and the data one finds outside the Scriptures. *One should constantly attempt to see the Bible as-a-whole and life as-a-whole.* If the reader has been impressed with the need for such a correlative attitude, then the preceding discussion has accomplished its major purpose.

V. EXERCISE ON CORRELATION

Attempt to find the relations which exist between the passages interpreted and applied in connection with preceding exercises. Also make an effort to relate these passages to what you see and hear and read outside the Scriptures.

NOTES

1. Ante, pp. 138-141, 156-159, 206-209.
2. Ante, pp. 6-8. The inductive movement from particulars to generalizations is applicable in two areas: first, in the study of single passages, where it involves observing the individual elements of a unit before drawing conclusions as to its meaning; and second, in the study of the entire Scriptures, where it concerns the examination of particular passages before making generalizations about the Bible as-a-whole. Induction was employed in the first area in the sections on observation and interpretation. The present emphasis on generalizations or correlation involves the second area.
3. Note that correlation is so described here as to include application.
4. Ante, p. 11.
5. In developing a Biblical theology, one should keep in mind the fact that an accurate correlation of Scriptural statements not only reflects the various individual doctrines contained in the Scriptures, but also the emphasis given to particular doctrines. For in a sense one's theology could include all the doctrines found in the Scriptures and at the same time be basically anti-Scriptural because of a misplaced emphasis. One should therefore make an effort to note those doctrines to which the most amount of material is devoted and which are considered basic by Biblical writers, and let such doctrines be fundamental in one's own correlation.

SUMMARY

At the outset of this study reference was made to John Dewey's definition of "method," in which he indicated its concern with "the crucial points where conditions of growth have to be carefully maintained and fostered." [1] Using this as a basis for surveying the preceding discussion, one may review it in seven simple words: see, inquire, answer, summarize, evaluate, apply, and associate.

The first crucial point of methodical study is to learn to *see*. For observation is the link between the subject and the object. Through it the mind becomes aware of the components of a passage, and induction thus has its beginning.

The major components of a passage are four in number: terms, structure, general literary forms, and atmosphere. These, then, should be the objects of the seeing eye. This is especially true of structure, which is so important in literary communication and yet is perceived only by the observer who diligently searches for it. [2]

But to become aware is not enough. The purpose of awareness is to supply the mind with the stuff on which to work. And this work begins when the mind *inquires* into the meaning of that which it has perceived. This therefore is a second crucial point where growth needs to be maintained and fostered. For unless curiosity and inquisitiveness are developed, the results of observation will be like fruit which is picked but not eaten.

However, inquiries in turn are helpful only if one attempts to *answer* them, and if one succeeds in answering them properly. This can be accomplished only through the development of the re-creative attitude, which causes one to stand in the shoes of Biblical authors in order to feel as they felt and to think as they thought. And whatever exegetical practices and aids are used should be employed in such a way as to promote re-creation.

When these re-creative answers have been made, then one's task is to integrate and *summarize* them in order to discover the primary message of an author. This step is crucial because of the very nature of a passage, which consists of a number of interrelated elements upon which an author depends for the communication of his ideas. Thus if one is to discover his message, one must interrelate one's interpretations of the various elements used in the passage.

The next crucial step involves the need to *evaluate* the message of a passage. For one must discover its exact worth and relevance before one will know how to benefit by it. This is necessary because the various parts of the Scriptures were written in and addressed to concrete historical situations which span hundreds of years. An effort must therefore be made to determine which truths are local and which are of universal value on the basis of the universal Christ.

When universal truth has been discovered, one should then find the situation to which the truth is relevant. And to such a situation one must *apply* the truth, not only in theory but also in actual practice.

When one has thus studied several passages, one is ready to begin a task which should occur continuously during one's lifetime. This task is to *associate* the passages one studies with each other and with the extra-Biblical data of experience. In this way one will develop a Biblical theology and ultimately a correlated Biblical view of life. This is the proper culmination of induction.

These, then, are the crucial steps of methodical Bible study which need to be maintained and fostered. And there is only one person in the world who is able to maintain and foster them. That is *you*. In your hands lies the decision as to whether you will train yourself in such a way so that God's Spirit can use you in the interpretation of the Scriptures. This book has merely been suggestive. It contains some guide-posts which point out the *methodos* to a fruitful study of the Bible. Now all depends on the traveler!

NOTES

1. Ante, p. 5.
2. Ante, p. 37.

APPENDIX

APPENDIX A

CHARTS

1. Kinds of Charts

Charts may be classified in two categories: *horizontal* charts and *vertical* charts. There are variations of both of these, but they represent the main types of charts. The former is most useful in connection with passages where perspective is important, such as larger units of material; the latter is frequently helpful in the study of shorter units, such as segments.

The horizontal chart may be drawn thus:

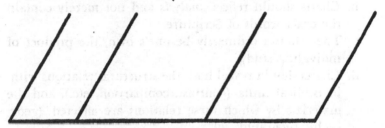

The vertical chart may be represented in the following way:

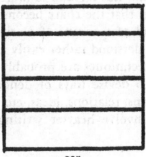

2. **Primary Reasons for Charts**
   a. They take advantage of the eye-gate and thus utilize another avenue of learning.
   b. They supply a helpful means for recording one's discoveries.
   c. They help to give one an impression of the framework and outstanding ideas of the whole.
   d. They provide a basis for teaching large units of material in a limited amount of time.

3. **Underlying Principles and Concrete Suggestions for Making Charts**
   a. One should be careful to keep charts *inductive*. The chart should be determined by the structure of Biblical material; the structure of Biblical material should not be determined by the chart. Do not force an idea upon a unit simply because it provides good material for a chart. Remember that the chart is a means and not the end.
   b. Charts should reflect *analysis* and not merely contain the exact words of Scripture.
   c. They should ordinarily be one's own, the product of individual study.
   d. Charts should reveal both the structural relations within Biblical units (contrast, comparison, etc.), and the materials by which these relations are effected (geography, biography, etc.).
   e. They should contain only *major* terms, relations, ideas, etc. One should not include so much material or draw so many lines that the chart becomes a source of confusion instead of a means of clarification. If a chart cannot be understood rather easily a year after its production, its techniques are probably fallacious.
   f. One ought to devise ways of denoting the *most important* sections, relations, ideas, etc. of a Biblical unit. These may involve heavier writing, underlining, or encircling.

g. Charts should be *synthetical* in nature and purpose; they should not simply indicate the distinct parts or divisions of a passage.

h. One should attempt to *vary* the ways in which one makes charts.

i. Charts should be *continuous* in order to accomplish their purpose of helping to foster perspective. If a chart is horizontal, for example, it should not be divided into two sections and one placed below the other.

j. Charts should *not be too long,* for excessive length also hinders perspective.

k. Charts should be so framed as to be readable from *one vantage point.* The full value of a chart cannot be realized if one finds it necessary to look at it from various angles so as to read it.

l. One should include *references* in one's charts. For example, chapter and verse indications should be noted in regard to Biblical material. If extra-Biblical quotations are used, their sources should be included.

m. It is often helpful to put the *theme* which is revealed in and by the chart at the top of the page.

n. Charts should be framed in such a way that others can read them. They should be *self-explanatory.* If necessary, one can indicate a legend which will serve as a guide. However, charts should be made as simple as possible.

o. The chart should reflect *message* as well as form. It should be interpretive as well as observational.

p. If possible, one should try to make the divisions of charts *proportionate* in length to the amount of Biblical material which they represent. In other words, if a structural unit of a passage consists of ten chapters, more space should be given to it than to one which is two chapters in length.

q. In charting it is generally best to follow the *chronological order* of the text and not to rearrange it.

r. Use *other visual aids* besides charts, such as outlines. Avoid becoming a slave of charts.

4. Other Contents of Charts

There follow some suggestions of other features which at one time or another may be included in a chart. Some may appear in the chart proper and others below it.

a. Chapter or paragraph titles.

b. Comparison and contrast of beginning and end of book.

c. Word studies.

d. Outstanding features not otherwise indicated.

e. Historical information, such as dates.

f. Analytical outlines of paragraphs or segments.

g. Maps.

h. Topical or biographical studies.

i. Good quotations—Biblical or extra-Biblical.

j. Problems for future investigation.

k. Topics for future study.

l. Main lessons (application).

m. Verses for memorization.

n. Devotional passages.

o. Sermonic suggestions.

p. Possible teaching approaches.

q. Correlation with other passages.

5. Examples of Charts

The following charts by no means fully illustrate the principles and suggestions of the preceding discussion. However, it is hoped that they will help clarify some essential points regarding charting, as well as indicate the structure of selected smaller and larger units of Biblical material.

a. *Psalm 23*[1]

A Psalm of Confident Trust

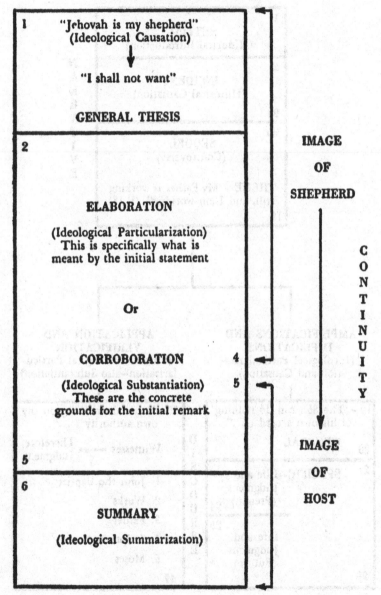

b. *John 5*

The Oneness of Father and Son

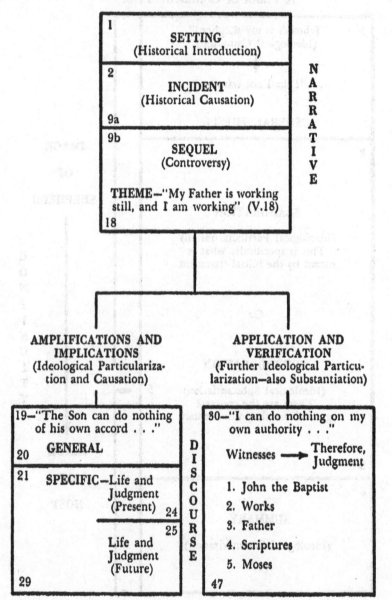

N A R R A T I V E

1
SETTING
(Historical Introduction)

2
INCIDENT
(Historical Causation)
9a

9b
SEQUEL
(Controversy)

THEME—"My Father is working still, and I am working" (V.18)
18

AMPLIFICATIONS AND IMPLICATIONS
(Ideological Particularization and Causation)

APPLICATION AND VERIFICATION
(Further Ideological Particularization—also Substantiation)

D I S C O U R S E

19—"The Son can do nothing of his own accord . . ."
20 **GENERAL**
21 **SPECIFIC**—Life and Judgment (Present) 24
25 Life and Judgment (Future)
29

30—"I can do nothing on my own authority . . ."

Witnesses ⟶ Therefore, Judgment

1. John the Baptist
2. Works
3. Father
4. Scriptures
5. Moses

47

c. *James 2*

The Works of Faith

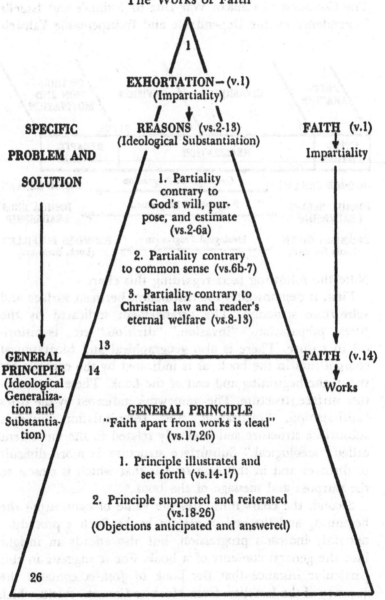

EXHORTATION — (v.1)
(Impartiality)

SPECIFIC   REASONS (vs.2-13)   **FAITH** (v.1)
(Ideological Substantiation)
PROBLEM AND

SOLUTION   1. Partiality   Impartiality
contrary to
God's will, pur-
pose, and estimate
(vs.2-6a)

2. Partiality contrary
to common sense (vs.6b-7)

3. Partiality contrary to
Christian law and reader's
eternal welfare (vs.8-13)

GENERAL   **FAITH** (v.14)
PRINCIPLE
(Ideological   Works
Generaliza-
tion and
Substantia-
tion)   **GENERAL PRINCIPLE**
"Faith apart from works is dead"
(vs.17,26)

1. Principle illustrated and
set forth (vs.14-17)

2. Principle supported and reiterated
(vs.18-26)
(Objections anticipated and answered)

d. *Joshua*

The Conquest of Canaan Was Due to Joshua's and Israel's Dependence on the Dependable and Indispensable Yahweh

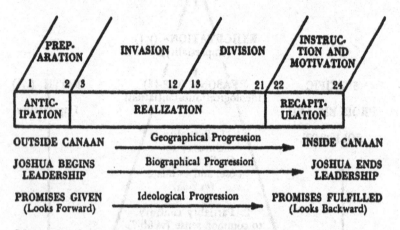

Note the following facts regarding this chart.

First, it demonstrates the distinction between surface and subsurface structure. The arrangement indicated by the titles "preparation," "invasion," "division," etc., is historical in nature. There is also geographical and biographical composition in the book, as is indicated by the contrast between the beginning and end of the book. These all constitute surface structure. The framework indicated by the titles "anticipation," "realization," and "recapitulation" involves subsurface structure and is closely related to the movement called "ideological." Subsurface structure is more difficult to discover and in this case reveals that which is closest to the purpose and message of the book.[2]

Second, the chart illustrates the value of contrasting the beginning and the end of certain books. Such a procedure not only indicates progression, but also affords an insight into the general contents of a book. For it suggests in this particular instance that the book of Joshua contains the journey of the Israelites from Moab to Canaan, events which occurred during the leadership of Joshua, and incidents in which God fulfilled the promises He made.[3]

Third, the chart indicates both structural relations and the materials which were used to effect them.

e. *I Samuel*

Two Ways of Life

(Biographical Contrast)

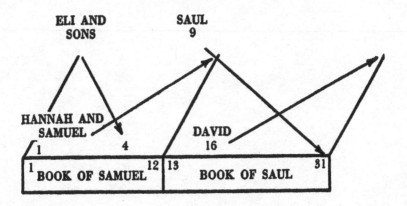

Biographical Contrast by Interchange

(I Samuel 1-12)

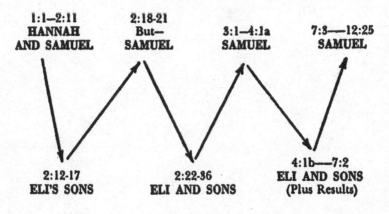

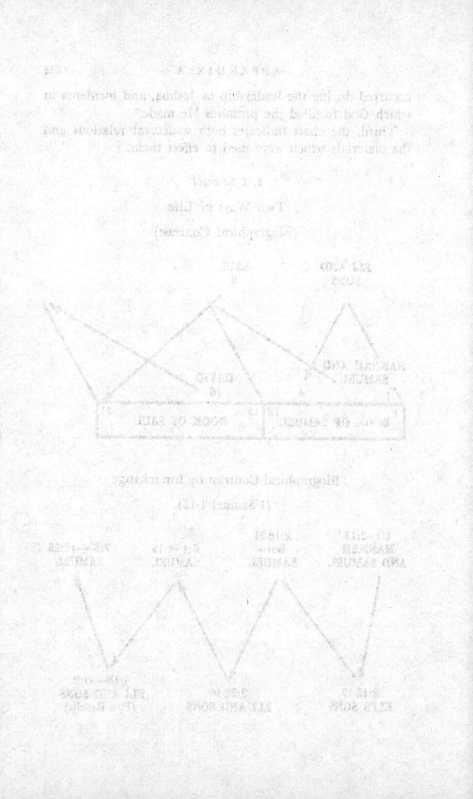

APPENDIX B

WORD STUDY: "HOLY" (*KADASH*)

The following material is far from exhaustive, but it is hoped that it will be suggestive both in regard to the approach and the values involved in word studies.

1. Etymology

(Sources: Hebrew lexicons, such as that of Gesenius; word studies like that of Girdlestone; Bible dictionaries, like the *International Standard Bible Encyclopedia;* English dictionary; miscellaneous sources, such as the *Jewish Encyclopedia.*)

a. *Root Meaning*

The original meaning of *kadash* is open to question. However, the view which seems to have the most in its favor is that *kadash* initially possessed the idea of separation or withdrawal. In this sense it was used to describe ceremonial objects which were withdrawn from common use. It was also employed to designate heathen deities, since gods are set apart or are different from men. *Kadash* seems to be used in its original sense in Deuteronomy 22:9.

b. *Derivative Significance*

From this root is derived the Old Testament concept of holiness or sacredness. That is holy which is withdrawn

245

from common use for employment in relation to God. Such a separation is necessary because Deity is involved. For since Deity is unique, that which is related to Deity must also be unique.

2. Usage [4]

(Sources: concordances, besides those mentioned above.)

The procedure followed in relation to this aspect is to examine all the references where the various forms of a word are used, trying to classify them if classification is possible. On the basis of the various types of uses as well as the use which is predominant, one can discover the basic way in which a word is employed. One should remember, however, that in the last analysis each term must be interpreted in the light of its individual context.

a. *Applied to Places*

(1) ". . . God called him out of the midst of the bush and said . . . put off thy shoes from off thy feet, for the place whereon thou standest is *holy* ground." (Exodus 3:4-5)

(2) "And let them make me a *sanctuary*, that I may dwell among them." (Exodus 25:8)

(3) "For Jehovah thy God walketh in the midst of thy camp . . . therefore shall thy camp be *holy*, that he may not see an unclean thing in thee, and turn away from thee." (Deuteronomy 23:14)

(4) "All the Levites in the *holy* city were two hundred fourscore and four." (Nehemiah 11:18)

(5) "Yet I have set my king upon my *holy* hill of Zion." (Psalm 2:6)

(6) "Now know I that Jehovah saveth his anointed; He will answer him from his *holy* heaven." (Psalm 20:6)

b. *Applied to Things*

    (1) "He [Aaron] shall put on the *holy* linen coat . . . they are the *holy* garments . . ." (Leviticus 16:4)

    (2) "But in the fourth year all the fruit thereof shall be *holy*, for giving praise unto Jehovah." (Leviticus 19:24)

    (3) "These also did king David *dedicate* unto Jehovah . . . " (II Samuel 8:11)

    (4) "And they brought up the ark, and the tent of meeting, and all the *holy* vessels that were in the Tent . . ." (II Chronicles 5:5)

    (5) "I [God] have found David my servant; with my *holy* oil have I anointed him." (Psalm 89:20)

c. *Applied to Times*

    (1) "And God blessed the seventh day and *hallowed* it; because that in it he rested from all his work which God had created and made." (Genesis 2:3)

    (2) "In the first day ye shall have a *holy* convocation: ye shall do no servile work." (Leviticus 23:7)

    (3) "*Sanctify* a fast, call a solemn assembly, gather the old men and all the inhabitants of the land unto the house of Jehovah your God, and cry unto Jehovah." (Joel 1:14)

d. *Applied to People*

    (1) With *man* as active agent

        (a) "*Sanctify* unto me all the first-born, whatsoever openeth the womb among the children of Israel, both of man and of beast; it is mine." (Exodus 13:2)

        (b) "And thou shalt put them [coats, girdles, headtires] upon Aaron thy brother, and upon his sons with him, and shall anoint them, and con-

secrate them, and *sanctify* them, that they
may minister unto me in the priest's office."
(Exodus 28:41)

(c) "For I am Jehovah your God; *sanctify* yourselves therefore, and be ye *holy;* for I am holy:
neither shall ye defile yourselves with any
manner of creeping thing that moveth upon
the earth." (Leviticus 11:44)

(d) "Speak unto all the congregation of the children of Israel, and say unto them, Ye shall be
holy; for I Jehovah your God am holy." (Leviticus 19:2)

(2) With *God* as active agent

(a) ". . . Verily ye shall keep my sabbaths . . .
that ye may know that I am Jehovah who *sanctifieth* you." (Exodus 31:13)

(b) "And ye shall keep my statutes, and do them:
for I am Jehovah who *sanctifieth* you." (Leviticus 20:8)

(c) ". . . before thou camest forth out of the
womb I *sanctified* thee; I have appointed thee
a prophet unto the nations." (Jeremiah 1:5)

e. *Applied to God*

(1) In describing His relation to men

(a) ". . . and I will be *sanctified* in you in the
sight of the nations." (Ezekiel 20:41)

(b) "And I will *sanctify* my great name, which
hath been profaned among the nations, which
ye have profaned in the midst of them; and the
nations shall know that I am Jehovah, saith
the Lord Jehovah, when I shall be *sanctified*
in you before their eyes." (Ezekiel 36:23)

(2) In describing His character

(a) His Incomparableness—"To whom then will

ye liken me, that I should be equal to him?
saith the *Holy* One." (Isaiah 40:25)

(b) His Unapproachableness—"And the men of
Beth-shemesh said, "Who is able to stand before
Jehovah, this *holy* God? . . ." (I Samuel 6:20)

(c) His Deity—"I will not execute the fierceness
of mine anger, I will not return to destroy
Ephraim: for I am God, and not man; the
Holy One in the midst of thee . . ." (Hosea
11:9)

(d) His Sublimity—"For thus saith the high and
lofty One that inhabiteth eternity, whose name
is *Holy:* I dwell in the high and holy place,
with him also that is of a contrite and humble
spirit. . . ." (Isaiah 57:15)

(e) His Moral Purity—"And [the seraphim] . . .
cried one to another, and said, *Holy, holy,
holy* is Jehovah of hosts. . . . Then said I
[Isaiah], Woe is me! for I am undone; because
I am a man of unclean lips, and I dwell in the
midst of a people of unclean lips: for mine eyes
have seen the King, Jehovah of hosts." (Isaiah
6:3, 5)

3. **Partial Summary of Findings**

a. *Primary Meaning*—a *Relation* (based both on etymology and on predominance in usage)

(1) Stated negatively—separation from that which is
common. (Exodus 3:4-5, Psalm 89:20, Ezekiel
20:41, Hosea 11:9)

(2) Stated positively—dedication or consecration to
God's service. (Exodus 13:2, II Samuel 8:11, Jeremiah 1:5) [5]

b. *Implied Meaning*—a *Quality* (moral purity). (Leviticus 11:44, Deuteronomy 23:14, Isaiah 6:3, 5)

c. *Their Connection*

In order to be qualified for God's service, which is the purpose of holiness in relation to places, things, times, and persons, there must be a separation from that which is commonly not employed in God's service and a dedication to God. But because the common condition is uncleanness, withdrawal from that which is common entails cleansing. And further, since God is set apart from sinful men and is therefore morally pure, only that which has been purified is fit to be used in His service. Thus the primary meaning supplies the cause of which the implied meaning is the inevitable effect. Separation unto God involves cleansing.[6]

APPENDIX C

LOGICAL OUTLINES

1. Description of Logical Outlines

The logical outline is basically different from the topical outline. The latter concerns various parallel aspects of one topic. For example, if a topical outline were being formulated on the subject of "New York City," some of its main divisions might be "Its Largeness," "Its Centrality," and "Its Cosmopolitanism." Now it is true that these phases are related to each other, but they are distinct enough so that they may be treated as separate features. On the other hand, the logical outline involves *successive* and *interdependent* steps, each of which is grounded upon that which precedes. Such an outline is *argumentative* in nature; it attempts to prove something. It denotes *logical development*. It does not merely describe a topic; it *supports* a conclusion.

2. Use of Logical Outlines

In view of the preceding description of a logical outline, it is apparent that this type of outline is especially helpful in the study of the ideological type of literature, such as one finds in the Epistle to the Romans or the Epistle to the Hebrews.

One should be aware that this type of outline is merely a *means* of coming to grips with the logic of a unit of literature. Its use does not imply that the author of a passage or book had an outline in mind which he slavishly followed in his writing. It simply serves as a tool by which to trace logical development, to discover how various thoughts are related to each other, to determine what is primary and what is secondary, and to ascertain the conclusion toward which the author is moving.

It should further be noted that the logical outline is an *imperfect* means. It has its shortcomings, as one soon discovers when one uses it to any great degree. However, it seems to be the best instrument which can be used to bring one face to face with the development and force of a logical passage.

3. Suggestions for Making Logical Outlines

  a. Use the sentence form of outlining, since the force of an argument can be conveyed only by full statements.

  b. Analyses in terms of purpose, basis, result, etc., may be placed in parentheses after the various statements of the outline. They should not in themselves constitute the points of the outline.

  c. Indicate clearly and cogently the *relations* between ideas in one or both of the following ways: first, by position, since, for example, a subordinate position indicates a subordinate idea; and second, by connectives and connections, such as "therefore," "for," "because," "for this reason," or dependent and independent clauses. These relations should be so expressed so as to result in actually proving what the author is proving.

  d. At the head of each outline there should be stated in proposition form the theme of the passage. Such a theme should reveal among other things the logical relation of the passage to its immediate context and its purpose in the movement of the book as-a-whole. Sometimes such a theme is explicitly stated, and in other instances it is implied. In both cases the theme should be discovered and noted. One should be careful that the theme is found through induction and not superimposed on the passage. The outline should demonstrate the logical steps which the Biblical writer follows in substantiating his theme.

e. As was indicated in the preceding suggestion, a logical outline must include both that which is explicit and that which is implicit in a unit. One must read between the lines if one is to catch the full force of the argument of a logical passage. However, one must be careful to base one's conclusions on objective data and not on pure imagination.[7]

f. Follow the order of the text so as to avoid the danger of altering its logic. Sometimes it makes no substantial difference if one varies the order of the text. At other times serious changes may result. Therefore, the safe practice is to follow the exact arrangement of the passage.

g. Be *thorough* in your outlining, for the thoughts of certain portions of Scripture are so closely knit together that to omit one is to cause a serious gap in the argument. It is better to be too thorough, if that is possible, than not to be thorough enough.

h. Use the regular outline form—I, A, 1, a, (1), (a), etc. Do not use a "I" unless it is followed by a "II", an "A" unless followed by a "B," etc. For outlining involves setting down two or more aspects of one thing. If there are not at least two aspects of the idea being considered, then it should not be outlined. Therefore, if, for example, one places an "A" under an "I" without a corresponding "B," one should combine the "A" with the "I."[8]

i. *Use your own language.* Avoid the mere repetition of the terminology of the text.

j. A logical outline should serve two purposes: *synthesis* and *analysis.* The major points, especially "I" and

"A," should be synthetic. For example, the Roman numerals should represent the greatest possible synthesis of similar ideas in relation to a certain theme. On the other hand, the more minor points should represent the analytical aspect of the outline. They should contain the individual arguments which are woven together so as to support the more major arguments and the theme.

k. Avoid dividing statements into too many small parts because of the danger of losing the element of continuity; on the other hand, avoid combining too many ideas into one statement because of the danger of missing the importance of each.

l. Indicate chapter and verse references after your major points.

m. Prepare an outline only after thorough study, and let it be a means of summarizing your study. If one has studied a passage well, it ought to fall into an outline of its own accord. One should not be concerned about outlining as such in the process of interpretation.[9]

4. Examples of Logical Outlines

a. *Example of a Detailed Outline* (Romans 1:18-32)

Theme:

The Gentiles need the gospel of salvation, since, having the truth about God through revelation, they deliberately suppressed it because of their disrespect for Him and are therefore the objects of His wrathful and just judgment. (v. 18) [10]

I. For they have the truth about God, since God has plainly revealed it to them; they are therefore without the excuse of ignorance. (vs. 19-20) (REVELATION—CONSEQUENT RESPONSIBILITY)

A. For that which can be learned about God, namely,

His existence and nature, can be discerned by them,
since God has consciously and clearly shown it to
them. (v. 19—Fact of Revelation)

1. This has been true ever since the foundation of
   the world, since creation is the means by which
   God has disclosed Himself to them. (v. 20a—Substantiation—Time and Means of Revelation)
2. For through creation, which may be seen, the
   unseen character of God, that is, His everlasting
   might and other-than-manness, has been made
   plainly visible. (v. 20b—Further Substantiation
   —Content of Revelation)

B. Because of this plain manifestation of God's existence and nature, they cannot excuse their actions
   on the basis of a lack of knowledge. (v. 20c—Purpose
   and Outcome of Revelation—Responsibility)

II. Because, although they were given a conspicuous reve-
    lation of the truth about God, they deliberately re-
    pressed it and refused to act in accordance with it. (vs.
    21-23—REJECTION AND RETROGRESSION)

A. Instead of paying the admiration due to God because of His manifested grandeur, and instead of
   being grateful to Him for His provisions, they refused to worship Him or give Him thanks. (v. 21a—
   Contrast—Lack of Worship—First Step in Decline)

B. They rather became ineffectual in their thinking,
   since they attempted to reason without a Divine
   postulate. The result was utter confusion in their
   innermost beings. (v. 21b—Contrast—Darkened Intellect and Heart—Second Step in Decline)

C. As a consequence, they were completely self-de-
   ceived, claiming to be wise whereas they were actually fools; and the depth of their folly is shown by
   the fact that they exchanged the majestic splendor

of the true, incorruptible God for the mere like-
nesses of corruptible men, birds, four-footed beasts,
or even creeping things. (vs. 22-23—Result—False
Worship—Third Step in Decline)

III. Because they had a plain revelation of God and deliberately suppressed it, He judged them by removing
the restraining power of conscience and reason and
surrendering them to their own corrupt desires and
depraved minds. (vs. 24-32—RETRIBUTION—RE-
SULT)

A. God delivered them to the power of the lusts of
their hearts (vs. 24-25—Result)

1. This resulted in uncleanness, specifically involving the mistreatment of their bodies among
themselves. (v. 24—Subsequent Result)

2. God's surrender of them to their desires together with its consequences, I repeat, came
about because they exchanged the true God, the
God of everlasting power and divinity, for gods
who have no corresponding realities, and because
they adored and served the creature rather than
the Creator, who alone deserves praise. (v. 25—
Repetition of Reason)

B. Because they exchanged the true God for false gods
and creatures for the Creator, God delivered them
to the power of their shameful passions. (vs. 26-27—
Repetition of Reason and Further Result)

1. As a consequence, their women exchanged normal for abnormal sexual practices. (v. 26b—Result)

2. Similarly, men too engaged in unbridled and
ignominious acts of homosexuality, the results
of which constituted their rightful judgment. (v.
27—Similar Result)

C. And again, I repeat, since they deliberately refused to approve and admit God in their thinking, God also delivered them to the power of a reprobate and degenerate mind, and thereby to all manner of irrational and unfit conduct, both personal and social. (vs. 28-32—Repetiton of Reason and Further Result)

1. They were thus filled with all kinds of injustice, wickedness, covetousness, malignity. They are full of envious discontent, mortal hatred, contentiousness, falsity, evilness of mind. They are whisperers, false accusers and backbiters, scorners of God, despiteful, arrogant, braggarts, inventors of injurious things, disobedient to parents, without understanding, agreement breakers, heartless, ruthless. (vs. 29-31—Result and Particularization)

2. In fact, so utterly depraved are they that, knowing well God's decree that those who deliberately commit these sins will inevitably and justly be condemned to death, they not only do these things themselves, but even clap their hands when others practice them. (v. 32—Further Result and Particularization) [11]

b. *Example of a Summary Outline* (Romans 2:1-3:8)

Theme:

The Jews also need the gospel of salvation. For judgment is universally based on actual character and deeds; and since the Jews, although having great privileges and claiming thereby to be teachers, are so morally deficient that the Gentiles blaspheme God because of them, and since they cannot be exempted through physical circumcision or self-justification, they too are under God's condemnation.

I. Judgment is *universally* based on *actual character* and
   actions. (2:1-16—GENERAL PRINCIPLE)

II. Since judgment is *universally* grounded on *actual char-
    acter* and *actions,* and you Jews, although having great
    privileges and because of them being certain that you
    are able to teach others, are so morally corrupt that the
    Gentiles blaspheme God because of you, you too, I say,
    are likewise under Divine condemnation. (2:17-24—
    SPECIFIC APPLICATION)

III. *Being guilty and under judgment,* you will not be de-
     livered from wrath either by appealing to the physical
     rite of circumcision or to any amount of intellectual
     evasion and rationalization. (2:25-3:8—REBUTTAL
     TO ANTICIPATED OBJECTIONS)

APPENDIX D

USE OF MANUAL IN TEACHING METHODICAL BIBLE STUDY

Since the approach presented in this manual is rather novel, it was felt that teachers reading this material might be interested in how the writer uses it for teaching methodical Bible study.

Before indicating this, the writer wishes to make it clear that there are many ways of employing this manual, depending on the objective and the requirements of concrete situations. There is therefore no implication in the following statements that there is only one correct means of utilizing it.

There is a fundamental principle, though, which one may safely assume to be universally valid, namely, that if *anything should be taught methodically, it is methodical Bible study*. To this all can and should subscribe. For to do otherwise is to negate the very thing one is attempting to accomplish by the means used for its accomplishment. On the other hand, if one is guided by the desire to be methodical, then the aforementioned variations in particulars will make no substantial difference.

The writer has employed the manual as a text in conjunction with the study of the Gospel by Mark, which because of its simple narrative style lends itself well to the teaching of inductive study. No attempt is made in the course to cover the entire Gospel. Rather the Gospel is utilized as an area

259

for demonstrating and practicing the various principles and steps of methodical study.

The course is divided into two major phases, each of which will now be discussed.

1. Survey of Manual

The opening part of the course is given to a preliminary reading of the manual. The objective of such a reading is not to enable the student to understand and absorb every statement in the book, for this is an impossibility in view of the nature of methodical study. On the other hand, its purpose is to accomplish two main goals.

The first aim is that of giving the student a bird's-eye view of the whole before he is asked to use the individual parts. This provides him with an organized and comprehensive concept of inductive study which is lacking when one is introduced to its steps in a piecemeal and unsystematic manner. The student will consequently be able to understand the place and function of each individual phase in relation to the others, and will thereby be enabled to practice each step more intelligently. For he will foresee the purpose of each step, since he knows what follows. He will enjoy benefits similar to those realized by the person who goes to the top of the Empire State Building and sees New York City as-a-whole before attempting to find his way around the city street by street.[12]

The second aim of a preliminary survey of the manual is to give the individual a body of knowledge which he can employ in his study. This function is comparable with providing a student of geometry with axioms and theorems which he can utilize in the solution of geometric problems. When the individual is later asked to observe, for example, he will know the meaning, purpose, and objects of observation, or at least he will know where they may be found. On the other hand, to ask a student to observe without having made him aware of the exact significance of observation or what it is that he should be observing is like asking him to solve geometric problems without a knowledge of the axioms and theorems of geometry.

This fact came as a rude shock to this writer several years ago during a course in methodical study. About half of the semester had transpired, in which time observation had been demonstrated and practiced. Then suddenly in the process of a class discussion a student asked, "What is observation?" And much to the writer's surprise the entire class joined the questioner and pled that they be shown *exactly* what observation meant and how it operated. This experience led the writer to re-examine critically his teaching approach, and his conclusion was that the student must be given certain specific definitions and concrete facts beforehand if class demonstrations and personal practice are to approximate their full potentialities.

How the manual material should be divided for this preliminary survey depends on the time given to a particular course. However, one should attempt to plan the reading in terms of the units of methodical study. If necessary, the section entitled "Some Erroneous Kinds of Interpretation" or certain other sections could be omitted from the first reading.[13]

While the manual is being surveyed by the students, the writer utilizes the class period to discuss and illustrate the material read in conjunction with a particular session. In so doing he is guided by two factors: first, those principles and practices which are most crucial, and second, the points which are the most difficult to understand. For instance, in relation to the first of these factors, while the students are reading the section on observation, the writer discusses the matter of structure and illustrates it from passages in the Gospel by Mark which cannot be studied during the course. In relation to the second, the questions of students often indicate some of those matters which are difficult for them to comprehend. This does not imply that all of their questions can and should be answered at the outset, for some require time in order that the student's understanding may develop.[14] However, there are some questions which the teacher should attempt to answer immediately. It is these which the writer considers in this initial stage.

2. Application of Manual to Selected Passages in the Gospel by Mark

After the student has surveyed the manual, he is then ready to employ the material in relation to the Gospel by Mark. This may be done in either of two ways: first, he may apply the entire manual to each passage, that is, engage in a complete study of each passage; or second, he may practice the application of each step of methodical study separately.

Both of these have their disadvantages as well as their advantages. However, because of the time factor and the nature of inductive study, it seems to the writer that the second of these approaches is most salutary in teaching the beginner how to study methodically.

The main reason for this judgment is that the first approach tends to encourage superficiality. For if in preparation for each class the student is required to observe, interpret, evaluate, apply, and correlate, it is obvious that he cannot do any of these thoroughly, and that consequently he will not develop the understanding and skill necessary to do any of them well. On the other hand, the second approach fosters a more thoroughgoing understanding of each step and the ability to execute it. With this as a foundation, the student can eventually develop a personal approach to Bible study which will be both practical and valid.[15] In view of this, the writer directs the class to practice each step of methodical study individually in relation to certain passages in Mark.

Therefore, the first several class periods following the survey of the manual are devoted to a combination of observation and the asking of interpretive questions.[16] Emphasis is placed on the two phases of observation: the analytical and the synthetical.[17] The greatest stress is placed on the second, which because of its nature is primarily concerned with structural observation.[18] During the class period the writer demonstrates the technique of observation in relation to the passage being studied. He also attempts to indicate the values of the observations made by showing how they form the basis for a more profound interpretation of the passage.

The next group of periods is devoted to interpretation proper, including the answers to interpretive questions and their integration. In accomplishing this it is deemed wise to select the most basic determinants of interpretation and concentrate on them individually rather than asking the student to utilize all of them in relation to each passage. For example, the factors involved in word studies may be stressed in connection with one class period. The matter of contextual relations as an interpretive determinant may be emphasized in another period. Though one may not be able to cover all the ingredients in this manner, the students will achieve a better grasp of those which are covered and have a more solid basis for utilizing those that are not covered than if they were asked to apply all the factors to each passage.

The writer devotes most of the class hours to these first two steps of study. Those that remain are given to evaluation, application, and correlation. The reason for this is the conviction that when observation and interpretation are done thoroughly and properly, the following steps are much more easily effected than otherwise.

The major disadvantage of this approach is involved in the fact that for the sake of variety and maintaining interest it is unwise to spend several periods on one passage in order to make a thorough methodical study of it. However, this disadvantage is not substantial for the simple reason that the students are clearly told that their conclusions are to be considered tentative, and that as a consequence it is not necessary to engage in an exhaustive study of each passage. Thus one may concentrate on observation in relation to one passage and on interpretation in relation to another.

It should be noted that the preceding statements include the use of the three major avenues of learning and teaching: precept, demonstration, and practice. The first is utilized primarily in connection with the reading of the manual, the second primarily in the class discussions, and the third primarily in the individual's private study. All three of these are necessary and must abide, but the greatest of these is the exercising which the individual does in his own personal study. In this connection the writer has often told his students that if he had to make a choice between their attending class and their doing the exercises outside of class, he would be coerced by the very nature of the subject to exhort them to do the latter. For in learning how to study the Scriptures methodically, there is no substitute for actual practice.[19]

NOTES

1. Some of the structural relations on this chart may be questioned, as indeed they were in the preceding exercise on Psalm 23. (Ante, pp. 111-128.)
2. Ante, pp. 38-39.
3. Ante, pp. 64-65.
4. The factor of translation is also involved here, since the vernacular is being used. In order to utilize this factor fully, one needs to compare various translations.
5. Though the negative and positive aspects of holiness are ultimately inseparable, as one can surmise from a study of the references given, it is helpful to attempt to distinguish between them.
6. If this study were thorough, it would also include an examination of *hagiazo*, the New Testament equivalent of *kadash*.

7. Ante, p. 184.
8. There are some who would not agree with this suggestion, and with good reason; however, the writer has found it to be the most practical approach.
9. Ante, p. 167.
10. Although the Gentiles are not explicitly mentioned in the passage, for various reasons its statements seem to involve a description of the non-Jewish world. Further, the idea of the need for the gospel is implicit in the opening connective of verse 18. In fact, verse 18 is a summary of 1:18-32 and therefore contains in essence the theme of the passage. The remainder of the unit forms the elaboration of this theme. Two main structural laws are thus operative, namely, ideological substantiation and particularization. In other units different means of composition are used. What these are must be discovered and utilized if valid logical outlines are to be formulated.
11. It should be noted that the movement of this outline represents the progress of human experience as well as that of logic. Other logical passages may not follow the order of experience, for they may move from effect to cause.
12. Ante, p. 14.
13. Ante, pp. 167-181.
14. Ante, p. 22.
15. Ante, pp. 20-21.
16. Ante, pp. 97-98, 129-130.
17. Ante, p. 72.
18. Ante, p. 229.
19. Ante, pp. 14-15, 230-231.

BIBLIOGRAPHY

The following list contains books not already mentioned and which are of special help in regard to methodical study. Some of them are discussions of general principles and others are specific studies based on the inductive approach. For other books in the general field of Bible study, the reader is urged to consult *A Bibliography of Bible Study for Theological Students,* which was prepared by the library of Princeton Theological Seminary.

The fact that certain books are recommended in this manual does not imply that the writer agrees fully with their viewpoints. However, the books suggested all have some value, and further, they afford one the opportunity of becoming acquainted with various points of view, an opportunity which the inductive student of the Scriptures should welcome.

It should also be re-emphasized that the bibliographical recommendations of this manual are merely suggestive. There are other books which are of equal or superior worth to those mentioned and which the reader may prefer. If so, he should by all means use them.

Almack, J. C., *Research and Thesis Writing*

Bailey, A. E., *Art and Character*

Black, Max, *Critical Thinking*

Blair, E. P., *The Acts and Apocalyptic Literature*
Briggs, C. A., *Biblical Study*

Clifford, C. W., *How To Study*
Coleridge, S. T., *Treatise on Method,* edited by Alice D.
   Snyder
Cooper, Lane, *Louis Agassiz as a Teacher*

Dewey, John, *How We Think*
Dudley, L., and Faricy, A., *The Humanities*

Fitch, J. G., *The Art of Questioning*

Gettys, J., *How To Enjoy Studying the Bible*
   How to Study Luke

Harper, W. R., *Introductory Hebrew Method and Manual*
Hinsdale, B., *The Art of Study*
Hollingsworth, Jane, *Discovering Mark*

Interpretation, A Quarterly Journal of Bible and Theol-
   ogy (especially the "Studia Biblica" in each issue)
Koussevitzsky, Serge, "Interpreting Music," *The Atlantic
   Monthly,* August, 1948
Kuist, H. T., *How to Enjoy the Bible*
   Micah—But As For Me
   "The Training of Men in the Christian Tradition,"
   Union Review, April, 1941

Life, "A Life Round Table on Modern Art," October 11,
   1948

Love, J. P., *How To Read the Bible*

McMurry, F. M., *How To Study and Teaching How To
   Study*
Miller, Donald G., *Isaiah*
Morgan, G. C., *The Study and Teaching of the English
   Bible*

Palmer, C., *Emmanuel* (Matthew)
   The Superiority of the Christian Religion (Hebrews)

Richardson, Allan, *A Preface to Bible Study*

Smith, W. M., *Profitable Bible Study*
Smyth, J. P., *How To Read the Bible*
Starbuck and Maddox, *College Readings for Inductive Study*
Steen, E. B., *That You May Know* (Luke)

Thomas, W. H. G., *Methods of Bible Study*
Torrey, R. A., *How To Study the Bible for Greatest Profit*

White, W. W., *How To Study*
   Inductive Studies in the Twelve Minor Prophets
   Studies in Old Testament Characters
   Ten Studies in Paul's Letter to the Philippians
   The Divine Library, Its Abuse and Use